COLLINS COBUILD

COLLINS Birmingham University International Language Database

English Course

Photocopiable

Tests

LHBEC

Diana Fried-Booth
with
Dave and Jane Willis

1 2 3

Collins ELT
8 Grafton Street
London W1X 3LA

COBUILD is a trademark of William Collins Sons & Co. Ltd

© William Collins Sons & Co. Ltd 1989

10 9 8 7 6 5 4 3 2 1

First published in 1989

Printed in Great Britain by Mackays of Chatham PLC, Chatham, Kent.

ISBN 0 00 370267 7

Design: Chi Leung
Artwork: Gillian Martin

This book is accompanied by a cassette ISBN 0 00 370314 2

COBUILD is the Collins Birmingham University International Language Database

Acknowledgements *(Figures in brackets refer to pages.)*

The publishers and authors are grateful to the teachers and students of the following schools who piloted the tests and provided sample answers for the Answer Keys and Mark Scheme: Cassia English Centre, Rome; ELS International Language Centre, Greenwich; English Teaching Company, Madrid; Escuela Oficial de Idiomas de Carabanchel, Madrid; Language Teaching Centre, University of Oxford; School of English Studies, Folkestone.

The publishers are grateful to the following for permission to use original material: *This Month In Bath* for advertisements(9); Trust Tours, Day Tours to Stately Homes, Castle and Gardens for advertisements (23); Hong Kong Tourist Association for advertisements (29); British Rail for *Conference Connection* (30); MRB for the British Nutrition Foundation for article (31); *Young National Trust Magazine* for Winter Festivals (36); Department of Transport for leaflet (37); Book Club Association by arrangement with Century Hutchinson for extract from *British Folk Customs* by Christina Hole, 1976 (44); Octopus Books Ltd for extracts from *Amazing Mysteries and Phenomenon* by Peter Eldin (45, 70); Early Times for articles (52, 53, 67); Joanne Williams/ *Times Educational Supplement* 17/2/89 for articles (59).

To the teacher

This resource book contains photocopiable tests for all three Levels of the Collins COBUILD English Course. Following the grouping of units in the Student's Books of the Course, there are three tests for each of Level 1 and 2, and four tests for Level 3.

Each test follows a similar format, and covers vocabulary and pronunciation; grammar; reading; writing, and listening. At Level 3, the reading section includes work on dictionary skills.

A complete test will take approximately one hour to administer. However, teachers may prefer to set the listening section separately; accordingly, this section is printed separately, on a maximum of two sheets.

Full answer keys and guidance on marking can be found on pages 74-87 of this book. Sample student answers are given for the first test of each Level (focus on writing section only), to illustrate the apportioning of marks. Teachers should note that these marks are intended for guidance only and they may wish to alter them to suit their own students' needs.

Teachers can record the total marks per section in a box, which is positioned on the right at the end of each section of a test.

Tapescripts of the cassette material are on pages 88-93 of this book.

Contents

Page

Level 1 Test 1

Focus on vocabulary and pronunciation

1   Complete the words for **people** in this list.

teacher,   friend,   sec......................,   per......................,   st......................,   wo......................

2   Complete this list.

Sunday,   M............................, ..., ..., ...,

............................, ...

3   Fill in the words in sentences **a – c**.

a   Maria's parents got .... in 1978.

married   finished   asked   closed

b   Maria .... her baby brother that he was the ...

said   liked   replied   told

c   .... baby in the world!

nicer   good   best   prettier

4   Complete the words for **different family relationships** in this list.

sister,   br................,   fa................,   hu................,   wi................,   dau................

5   Put a tick (✓) under the small black triangle.

A   ▲   B   ●   C   ■   D   ▲

6   Put a tick (✓) under the big white square.

A   ○   B   □   C   ▢   D   △

Fill in the words in sentences **7 – 12**.

nice   light   like

7   Would you put the .... on please?

8   Can I carry your bag? No thanks — it's very ....

9   She's wearing a .... blue blouse and black trousers.

10   What .... weather!

11   Alan and John look .... students.

12   Which word does not have the same sound? Write it down.

hello   no   north   road   ....

Focus on grammar

Complete sentences **1 – 4**.

There's   There are   Where's   Where are

1   .... twenty students altogether in my class.

2   .... my watch? Have you got it?

3   .... a big book on my desk.

4   .... some money for you in my bag.

5   Fill in the word.

Marco's got a key.

Isabella's got a key.

Marco and Isabella have .... got keys.

6   Fill in the words in the text.

an   a   it   the   in

Marco lives in .... small house; .... is not ....

expensive house but Marco's family is very happy there. .... house has ....

nice garden with a lot of trees .... the centre.

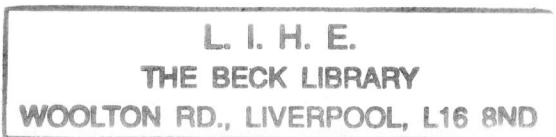

Focus on reading

Read the text and look at numbers **1 – 5**. Are they true or not true?
Write **true** or **not true**.

Richard lives in Bristol. He has a design agency where he works with his partner,
Philip. They are both married and have children. Richard has two sons and Philip
has a son and a daughter. Richard and his wife live in a big flat in central Bristol,
next to the office. Philip's family have a small house in the north of Bristol.

1   Richard and Philip work in Bristol.   ....

2   Richard has two daughters.   ....

3   Philip lives in the centre of Bristol.   ....

4   Richard and Philip each have the same number of children.   ....

5   Richard lives in a small flat.   ....

Read this dialogue between Monika and Pierre.

Answer questions **6 – 10**. Write **true** or **not true**.

6   Monika lives in a big house.   ....

7   Pierre lives alone.   ....

8   Monika thinks her house is nice.   ....

9   Pierre's house has a garden.   ....

10   Monika lives next to the school.   ....

Focus on writing

1 Look at the picture. Write about Marco's family.

....

....

....

....

....

....

....

2 What has Marco got on his desk?
Write three or four sentences.

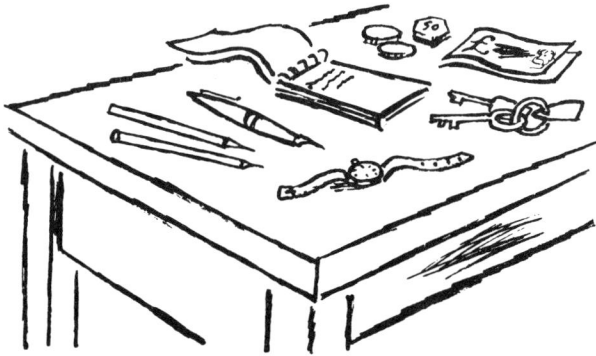

....

....

....

....

....

....

3 Look at the two pictures below.
Write down six differences, in note form.

....

....

....

....

....

....

....

....

....

Focus on listening

1   Fill in the information on the form.

WINSCOMBE SCHOOL OF ENGLISH

APPLICATION FORM

SURNAME   ....

FIRST NAME   ....

ADDRESS   ....

             ....

             ....

TEL: ....

---

2   Listen and complete the form for (a) – (f).

Apsley Estate Agents

CLIENT REQUIREMENTS

(a)   House ☐   Flat ☐   Cottage ☐   Bungalow ☐

(b)   Number of Bedrooms: 1 ☐   2 ☐   3 ☐   4 ☐   5 ☐

(c)   Kitchen ☐   Playroom ☐   Dining Room ☐   Laundry Room ☐

   Living Room ☐   Bathroom ☐

(d)   Central Heating ☐

(e)   Garden ☐   Garage ☐

(f)   Please note: ....

   ....

   ....

   ....

Level 1 Test 2

Focus on vocabulary and pronunciation

1   Match the words and numbers.

8,853	just over four hundred
3,002	under five hundred
407	just over seven thousand
476	over a thousand
1,169	about three thousand
7,091	almost nine thousand

Fill in the word in sentences **2 – 11**.

look   yourself   get   looks   place   myself   got

2   London's a very busy ....

3   I need someone to .... after my son for a few hours.

4   You .... very nice – is that a new hairstyle?

5   I bought .... a new coat last week.

6   What time do you .... up in the morning?

7   That car .... very old.

8   I've .... one brother and one sister.

9   Can I sit here or is this .... taken?

10   .... off the bus at the university.

11   Do you live by .... or with a partner?

12   One word in each set has a different sound. Put a line under it.

    a   walk   quarter   corner   each

    b   pretty   floor   British   women

© Collins ELT, 1989
COBUILD is a trademark of William Collins Sons and Company Limited

Focus on grammar

Fill in the words in **1** and **2** using **must** or **may**/**might.**

1   That .... be my book, it's got my name inside it.

2   Take your coat – it .... rain.

Fill in the words in **3** and **4** using **will** or **would.**

3   I .... love to go to China.

4   Can you be home by 6pm?   I .... try.

Put a line under the correct word to complete each sentence.

5   I know a place . . . you can buy cheap clothes.   (where/who)

6   . . . time do you finish work?   (who/what)

7   Do you know . . . to make a phone call in Britain?   (what/how)

8   . . . does David work for?   (when/who)

9   I left school . . . I was sixteen.   (how/when)

10   . . . shirt do you think is the nicest?   (who/which)

11   We're going to a restaurant . . . is not too far from here.   (what/which)

Fill in the words in **12 – 20**

    too   with   at   by   for   of   to

12   I've been a teacher .... 20 years.

13   These handicrafts were made .... people in the Third World.

14   Most people work from Monday .... Friday.

15   Where's Mike? He's .... the office.

16   I'm going to stay .... my friends for the weekend.

17   Have a look .... these photos – they're very good.

18   She did quite a bit .... work yesterday.

19   John's gone .... Bristol to see his sister.

20   If you eat .... much you'll feel ill!

Focus on reading

Answer questions **1 – 4** by writing the correct letter.

1 Which advertisement tells you where you can find a restaurant? ....

2 What would you phone to find out about travel costs? ....

3 What gives you information about buying books? ....

4 Where would you go to have something to eat? ....

A

🐦 **TUMI** 🐦

Latin American Craft Centres
THE LATIN AMERICAN LINK BRINGING
TWO WORLDS TOGETHER THROUGH FAIR TRADE
*Jewellery; Ceramics; Furnishing
Clothing and music*

● **8/9 New Bond Street Place,
Bath BA1 1BH (0225) 62367**

23, Chalk Farm Road,
Camden Town,
London NW1
01-485 4152

2 Little Clarendon St
Oxford OX1 2HJ
(0865) 512307

B

Top class live
music for all
business and
social functions.
Classical/popular/
dance/jass etc.

Contact: Virginia
Burton-Cooper,
30 Newlands Av.,
Radlett, Herts.
09276 5719

C

AIRLINE QUALITY AIR TRAVEL AT DISCOUNTED FARES

Special return airfares to
Sydney and Melbourne from £639
Perth from £579, Auckland from £739
New York from £249, Florida from £249
Los Angeles/San Francisco from £299
Atlanta/Houston/Dallas from £329
Toronto from £199

Specialists in all long-haul air travel as well as Europe.

Call now for a quotation whatever your destination.

Excellent first class and business class fares.

In England contact Airline, 6 Norfolk Street, Sunderland. Tel: 091-567 4717.

In USA contact 316-842 3515

With 20 years experience in the travel industry **we know our business.**

D

Ⓦ **WATERSTONE
& Company**

Have you been to Waterstone's lately?

We offer a wide range of books to suit every
interest and taste, general or academic.

E

**UNDER WOODS
COFFEE SHOP**

Full range of hot and cold food.
Salad Bar
Mon – Sat 9.30 am – 4.00 pm
Wed 8.30 pm – 4.00 pm
Great Western Antiques Centre, Bartlett Street

F

The General Trading Company

London's most fascinating shop has opened in Bath

Now you can find gifts from all over the world chosen for quality, style
and the quintessential Englishness for which the Company is best known.

10 Argyle Street, Bath. Telephone (0225) 61507

Shopping hours 9.00am to 5.30pm Monday to Saturday

G

**MENU
International**

A MENU GUIDE TO SOUTH DEVON
RESTAURANTS
OUT NOW – 95p
FROM ALL GOOD NEWSAGENTS

Read the passage about Laura and then write **true** or **not true** beside questions **5 – 9**.

Laura usually gets up at 8am with a cup of coffee to wake her up properly. She leaves home at 8.45 to reach the office at 9.30am. Then she starts work. She does a lot of things like writing letters, telephoning people and she often has to go out to see people at some point during the day.
She has a quick lunch at 1pm and she likes to get back home between 6pm and 7pm. In the evenings she likes to relax and sometimes she goes out to the cinema.
She's usually in bed by midnight, except on Saturday evenings when she goes out to a restaurant with friends.

5 Laura usually gets to work by 9am. ....

6 Laura often meets people during her working day. ....

7 Laura is usually home by 5.30pm. ....

8 Laura never goes out in the evenings. ....

9 On Saturdays Laura goes to bed after midnight. ....

Focus on writing

1   Using the information about the Polydor School of English find out about a course for yourself.
Say when you would like to go. Ask about the cost for a 4-week course and say what sort of classes
you would like. The letter has been started for you.

POLYDOR SCHOOL OF ENGLISH

LIVERPOOL

Summer Courses: 4 weeks

Levels: Beginners
        Intermediate
        Advanced

Starting dates: June 1st
        June 29th
        July 28th
        August 25th

Accommodation & meals:
Students live with local families.
Lunch is provided in the school Monday
to Friday. All other meals are taken with the
family.

The Director,
Polydor School of English,
1, New Street,
LIVERPOOL.

Dear Sir,

....

....

....

....

....

....

....

2   This is what David did last Saturday.

What do you usually do on a Saturday? Write about 50 words.

....

....

....

....

....

....

....

Focus on listening

1   Fill in the information.

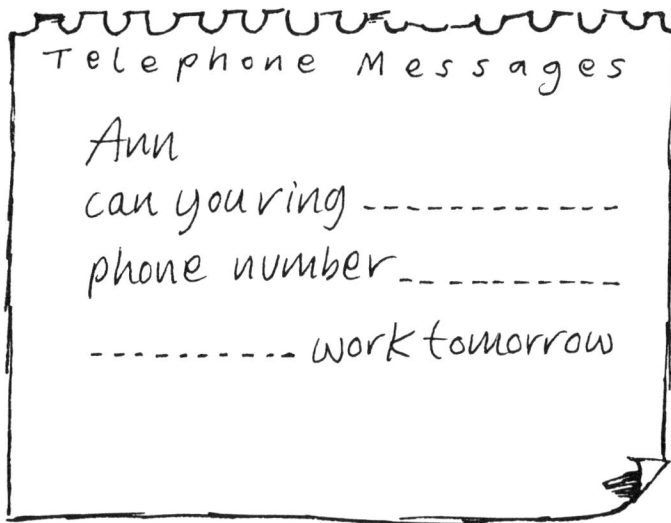

```
Telephone Messages

Ann
can you ring ------------
phone number ----------
----------- work tomorrow
```

Answer questions 2 – 4.

2   When is Howard's birthday?

   ....

3a   What time is it best to ring John?

   ....

b   Which day is John not at home?

   ....

4   Draw a line on the map to show how to get from Waverley Station to Moray Place.

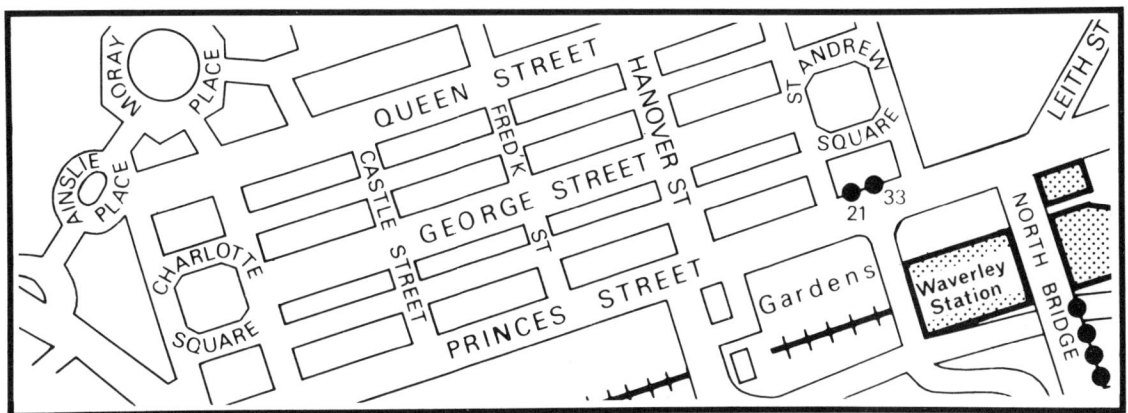

Level 1 Test 3

Focus on vocabulary and pronunciation

Fill in the gaps using the words below to help you.

see   over   keep   life

1   Visitors from all.................... the world come to London every year.

2   I'll .... you later on today.

3   How's .... these days?

4   This question is very difficult – I don't .... what you mean.

5   I hope to visit as many places as possible .... the next two weeks.

6   What film are you going to .... this evening?

7   Can you .... supper for me, I'll be late home.

8   I've lived in Manchester all my ....

9   You can't .... that money – it's not yours.

10   The River Nile is .... a mile wide in places.

11   Put a line under the word which does not have the same sound as the others.

staying   break   coast   take

12   What sound is the same in all these words? Put a line under it.

useful   Europe   you   unusual

Focus on grammar

1 Fill in the past tenses of these verbs. Example: get ....*got*.......

answer .... give .... come .... hear ....

is .... feel .... try .... explain ....

Put the words in the right order.

2 father at with staying is us present my

....

3 morning you did what arrive time this

.... ?

Fill in the words. Use **have/haven't**, **has/hasn't**, or **had**.

4 You look tired. Why don't you.................... a rest?

5 Would you like to .... lunch now or later?

6 I .... a good day at the office yesterday.

7 I'm sorry I .... written to you earlier.

8 He .... booked his ticket yet.

Put in the correct form of the words in brackets.

9 It looks a bit like Paris, ... ?   (doesn't it/isn't it)

10 It could be Russia .... ?   (can't it/couldn't it)

11 It isn't England .... ?   (is it/can it)

12 I don't think it's America .... ?   (does it/is it)

13 You've been to America............................... ?   (didn't you/haven't you)

Write your own sentences using these words.

Example: can: *Can I borrow your pen, please?*

14 going to: ....

15 if: ....

16 as: ....

17 so: ....

18 need: ....

Look at the sentences below. If you think **that** can be left out, put brackets around it.

Example: Take notes so (that) you will remember what happened.

19 That was a nice dinner.

20 I was so busy that I couldn't go on holiday.

21 The book on that table is mine.

Focus on reading

Read the letter below then answer questions **1 – 6** by putting **true** if you agree
with a sentence or **not true** if you disagree.

221, Sadler Street,
Tauntonville B.C.
2nd September.

Dear Claire,
　Many thanks for your last letter and the photos.
Ian looks almost as tall as you now, you must let
me know what he would like for his birthday next
month.
　It would be lovely to see you if you are able to
come to Canada next year. Do you know it's three
years since we last met! And I haven't seen Ian
since he was a baby!
　Anyway, if you're planning to come in August
I'll be on holiday, so perhaps we can spend a few days
together somewhere. I've a friend who's got a house
in Vancouver and I know she'd let us have it for a
few days. I've never been there but it sounds a great
place to stay. So let me know your plans.
Write soon!　Love Dawn.

　　　P.S. Don't forget to tell me
　　　　what I can get Ian!

1　Ian is taller than Claire.　　　　　　　　........................

2　It was Ian's birthday last month.　　　　　........................

3　Claire is planning to visit Canada.　　　　........................

4　Claire and Dawn last met three years ago.　........................

5　Dawn goes to Vancouver every August.　　........................

6　Claire's friend has a house in Vancouver.　........................

Focus on writing

	YOU	JOHN	LUCIA
COUNTRY?		England	America
WHO WITH?		Sister	Friend
HOW?		Sea	Air
WHEN?		October	June
HOW LONG?		1 week	2 weeks
PLANS?		Sport	Sight-seeing

1 You and some friends are planning your holidays. Fill in the table above with information for yourself and then write about **either** your plans **or** John's plans **or** Lucia's plans.

....

....

....

....

....

....

2 A friend is coming to stay in your home while you are away. Leave her/him a message about the things she/he will need to know such as keys, food and drink, neighbours, shops etc. The note has been started for you.

Hi! Welcome!
Please make yourself at home
Use the telephone if you need
to

Focus on listening

1   Put the list of things that Karl did in the right order.

saw a video	......
went to students' room	1
got homework	9
had a test	......
met the teachers	......
got textbooks	......
went to classroom	......
had lunch	......
had coffee	5

2   Listen to the message on Sue's answerphone and look at sentences **a – f**.
     Write **true** or **not true**.

a	Lisa is arriving on Wednesday	....
b	Lisa's brother lives in Edinburgh.	....
c	Lisa is first going to stay with Rosa.	....
d	Lisa might go to Exeter.	....
e	Lisa wants Sue to phone her.	....
f	Lisa is not at home before 10pm.	....

Level 2 Test 1

Focus on vocabulary

Use the following words to fill in the sentences.

clear   work out   bit   spend   about   clearly   time   look up

1   If you can just wait a .... I'll come into town with you.

2   Did you have a good .... on holiday?

3   Use a dictionary to .... the meanings of new words.

4   I saw a marvellous film last night called 'Moonbusters'!

    What was it .... ?

5   No teacher likes reading work which is not .... written.

6   Can you .... the cost of 10 books at £3.95 each?

7   See you later – I'll be back .... seven.

8   Do you know any Russian?

    I learnt a .... at school but I've forgotten it all now.

9   I hate flying – next .... I go abroad I'm going by train!

10 I was just .... to go out when the phone rang.

11 Can you explain this train timetable to me? It's not ....

    to me how it works.

12 What do you do in your spare .... ?

13 I'd love to come shopping with you but I mustn't .... too

    much money.

14 The sky was so .... you could see for miles from the hilltops.

15 I'd love to go to the concert but I'm afraid I haven't ....

Focus on grammar

1 Look at the picture and complete the text.

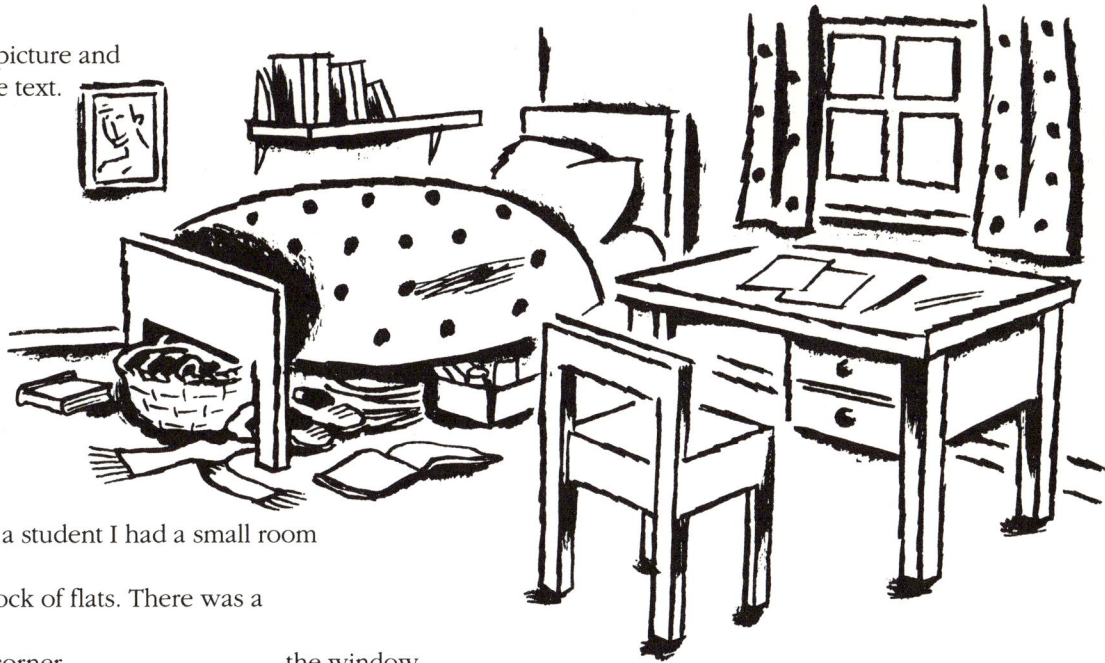

When I was a student I had a small room

in a large block of flats. There was a

bed in one corner .... the window,

and .... the window was

my desk. I kept my books ....

a shelf .... my bed and everything

else .... my bed!

Use the correct forms of the verb **be** to fill in sentences **2 – 6**.

2 I lived abroad when I .... a child.

3 My parents .... going to live in Australia when they retire.

4 Dominic .... 14 years old and goes to the local secondary school.

5 .... you going to the disco this evening?

6 When John and Susan .... first married they lived in a small flat.

Match the word on the left with the rest of the sentence.

7	What	☐	☐	do you live?
8	Who	☐	☐	days until the end of term?
9	Why	☐	☐	time shall we leave?
10	Where	☐	☐	asked you to come?
11	How many	☐	☐	are you sitting here by yourself?

12   Underline the correct word.

Xanthe and her brother live in Wells who / which / where is the smallest city in

England with a population of about 10,000. Xanthe, what / which / who is ten

years old, goes to a special music school where / why / which was built hundreds

of years ago. Children where / which / who go to a school like this have a musical

training as well as normal lessons.

Complete the sentences using the correct forms of the verb **have**.

13   .... you got any brothers or sisters?

14   Ben .... blue eyes and dark hair when he was a baby.

15   Elizabeth is .... six friends to her party.

16   .... anyone seen my bag?

17   I like our new English teacher very much – she .... a lovely sense of humour.

Underline the correct word.

18   I spent the morning at the market but couldn't find . . . worth buying.   (anyone/anything)

19   . . . who works at night should be well paid.   (anywhere/anyone)

20   Has . . . ever told you how beautiful you are?   (anything/anyone)

21   . . . must leave the examination room until I say so.   (somebody/nobody)

22   . . . had taken my dictionary and not given it back.   (somebody/everybody)

23 Use **and**, **so** or **but** to complete the text.

When Dominic was a small boy he had a bad accident. He was running along a

road where some workmen were digging a hole. The men were all very busy

.... they didn't see him coming. His parents who were walking along behind

him called out to him .... he suddenly disappeared from view! They quickly

ran to the spot where the workmen were .... found Dominic crying at the

bottom of a deep hole. He hadn't broken any bones .... he had cut his head

very badly .... he needed to go to hospital .... have ten stitches.

Write out sentences **24 – 27**.

24 written this Michael Rosen by poem was

....

25 was 1917 JF Kennedy in born

....

26 family run the Baxter hotel is the by

....

27 France being between is a England built tunnel and

....

Focus on reading

Put a tick (✓) if you agree with these statements.

1   If you stay in St Albans you won't be able to do much shopping.

2   There is a theatre in Tunbridge Wells.

3   Foreign visitors are not allowed to shop at the Scottish Woollen Mill Shop.

4   The Calverley Hotel is in the countryside.

5   St Albans has no rail routes.

6   It is best to book if you want to stay at St Michael's Manor Hotel.

7   The Scottish Woollen Mill Shop is in Scotland.

8   St Albans is a new town.

Read the text about John Mannion
and look at **9 – 14**. Are the
statements true or not true? Put a
tick (✓) next to the ones that are true.

9   Warrington offers beautiful country views.

10   Warrington is an attractive town.

11   John Mannion was quite successful at school.

12   John Mannion went abroad before going

   to university.

13   John Mannion enjoys various sports.

14   John Mannion spends most of his time talking.

> I was born in 1956 in Warrington Lancashire, which is a small industrial town in the north of England. It was not a very pleasant place to grow up in. I went to an all boys grammar school which I didn't enjoy very much, but I did quite well there. I went to Oxford University and studied English Literature and am now an English teacher in West London.
> After University I spent two years in Kenya and I still like to travel whenever I get the chance. I am not at all interested in sports but enjoy films, plays and bridge. I read a great deal and talk even more. I like people who can share my sense of humour.
> J.M.

Focus on writing

1   You are on holiday at the place in the picture. Write a
    postcard to your friends. Give them information about when
    you will return. You hope they are going to meet you when
    you arrive.

_____

_____

_____

_____

_____

_____

_____

_____

_____

2   You are applying for a job. Write a brief description of yourself –
    your interests, your character, any work experience you already have,
    and your ambitions for the future. Use about 100 words.

....

....

....

....

....

....

....

Focus on listening

1   Put a tick (✓) under the right pictures.

A   B   C   D

A   B   C   D

2   If you agree with the statement put a tick (✓).

a	The woman hasn't got any money.	....
b	The man offers to help the woman get a job.	....
c	The man has always had a good job.	....
d	The woman used to work in a hotel.	....
e	The hotel manager was very bad-tempered.	....
f	Working in a factory was bad for the man's health.	....
g	The man enjoyed working in an office.	....
h	His present job needs languages.	....
i	His present job is not very well-paid.	....
j	The man expects his wages will change next month.	....

Level 2 Test 2

Focus on vocabulary

Put a circle around the letter of the word that best completes the sentence.

1   My food bill was quite low this week – it only .... to £24.

    A went   B was   C got   D came

2   Take your umbrella just .... it rains.

    A in fact   B in time   C in order   D in case

3   Do you think you could .... me a glass of water, please?

    A mix   B pour   C stir   D melt

4   My parents wouldn't .... me go to a disco until I was 16.

    A let   B leave   C make   D take

5   I had a .... strange dream last night!

    A probably   B actually   C really   D simply

6   Have you .... been to Russia?

    A ever   B quite   C well   D very

7   The old man was attacked on his .... home from the cinema.

    A path   B direction   C movement   D way

8   The Prime Minister has .... his party to victory many times.

    A done   B led   C brought   D had

9   'I'd like you to .... me some advice on my investments,' John said.

    A have   B suggest   C give   D lend

10   Since joining the EEC Britain has done less .... with New Zealand.

    A post   B trade   C export   D order

11   Could you move your chair please – it's in my ....

    A route   B line   C way   D distance

12   Placido Domingo is one of the world's .... opera singers.

    A guiding   B moving   C pointing   D leading

© Collins ELT, 1989
COBUILD is a trademark of William Collins Sons and Company Limited

Focus on grammar

Complete the sentences with a suitable ending.

1   I was very tired after my journey and consequently ....

....

2   As a result of the plane crash ....

....

3   I am staying at home this evening because ....

....

4   It was raining very heavily so ....

....

5   I couldn't answer the phone as ....

....

Use words from the list to fill in the sentences.

off   up   by   below   behind

6   After his illness he didn't feel .... to returning to work.

7   My Japanese isn't very good but I can get ....

8   You are not allowed to vote in the UK .... the age of 18.

9   Can you turn .... the TV – I'm trying to read.

10   I grew .... in the north of England.

11   If you are interested in the job you must apply .... letter.

12   Peter isn't usually so kind – I think there must be something .... it.

13   The first road .... to the right is called Manor Park.

Underline the correct word to fit each sentence.

14   When I was a student I did .... jobs I could find.   (whatever/however)

15   I'll see you .... time you can make it.   (whenever/whatever)

16   I've never passed a music exam .... hard I've tried.   (whenever/however)

17   There's a prize for .... gets all the answers right.   (however/whoever)

18   .... it is you intend going you must let your boss know.   (whatever/wherever)

Put in the correct form of the verb.

19 I watched her train .... away until it disappeared from view.   (pull)

20 If I .... a lot of money I'd buy a larger flat.   (have)

21 Provided you .... not to drive too fast I'll lend you my car.   (promise)

22 You can get me at work by .... 867715.   (call)

23 I would give you a lift if I .... but I'm not going in your direction.   (can)

Put in the missing words.

24 You should call the police .... soon .... possible after a serious accident.

25 London is one of the best places .... concerts and plays.

26 Can you tell me .... much as you can remember about your childhood.

27 I rang the garage .... see if my car was ready.

28 These new boots are great .... walking.

Focus on reading

Look at this page of advertisements from a Hong Kong tourist newspaper and put a tick (✓) next to each statement if you think it is correct.

1   The Lotus Pond restaurant is not open for lunch.   ....

2   Jimmy's Kitchen offers guests a free drink with every meal.   ....

3   You can listen to live music at the Old Heidelberg Bar.   ....

4   Beggar's Chicken was originally cooked in a big saucepan.   ....

5   Service charges are included at the Mayur restaurant.   ....

6   A second Jimmy's Kitchen was opened in the sixties.   ....

7   The Old Heidelberg Bar is closed on Sundays.   ....

8   Beggar's Chicken is a dish from northern China.   ....

9   The Lotus Pond has an all-day parking service.   ....

10 Lunch and dinner prices are the same at the Mayur restaurant.   ....

Old Heidelberg

Come along and join the regulars at one of the best bars in town. The Old Heidelberg has a warm friendly atmosphere that makes you welcome and the staff will quickly make you feel like a regular.

Local and imported beer, wines and cocktails are available with happy hours from noon till 8.30pm. Snacks are available all day long with live music, entertainment and dancing nightly.

1st FLOOR, 24 ASHLEY RD,
TSIM SHA TSUI: 3 – 7233666
HOURS: NOON – 2am MON – SAT
5pm – MIDNIGHT SUN

MAYUR INDIAN RESTAURANT

LARGEST INDIAN RESTAURANT IN TOWN

Gourmet Curries of Indian Traditions
Best "TANDOOR" Dishes

Coastal seafood Specialities

Everyday Lunch Buffet 12.00 noon – 3.00
HK$40.00 plus 10% Service Charge

Dinner Buffet 6.00pm – 11.30pm
HK$60.00 plus 10% Service Charge

One glass of beer or soft drink
free with buffet

For Reservations Please Call: 3-675044-5
13/F., B.C.C. Building,
25-31 Camarvon Road,
Tsimshatsui, Kowloon, Hong Kong

Beggar's Chicken

This dish originated from the Hangzhou region in the northern areas of China and has only quite recently caught on with the southern Cantonese.
The story goes that an old begger felt extremely hungry one day and in desperation stole a live chicken from a farm. He managed to kill it but then realised he had no utensils with which to cook the bird so he desided on a bit of quick improvisation. First of all he gathered some lotus leaves from a nearby pond and wrapped the chicken up in these large leaves. He then used the mud from the lotus pond to wrap up the chicken. Next he lit a fire and set the chicken to bake on it. When he juged the bird was well cooked he found he had invented a tasty dish!

Lotus Pond

If you think you've tried Szechuen food you haven't. Unless you've eaten at Lotus Pond

At Lotus Pond we are proud to serve the traditional delicacies of true Szechuen cuisine. Our master chef, Mr. Tong Sui Lin, is the only Szechuen chef honoured with the Chaine des Rotisseures Award.

Come to Lotus Pond for the real experience in traditional Szechuen cuisine.

Open daily from
11a.m. to midnight.
15 Harbour City, Phase IV,
Ground floor
Canton Road, Kowloon.
Parking services
from 7p.m. to midnight.
For reservations
call: 3-7241088

Jimmy's Kitchen

The last thing Hong Kong needs is another restaurant.

That's what they told us back in 1928. But when you consistently give people fine European food, with friendly service, in a warm, cosy atmosphere, it works. In fact, it worked so well we opened a second one in 1969. The way we look at it, you can't have too much of a good thing.

Jimmy's Kitchen. Not just another restaurant. On both sides of the harbour.

Kowloon
1/F., Kowloon Centre,
29 Ashley Road, Tsimshatsui.
Tel: 3-684027
Hong Kong
1-3 Wyndham Street, Central.
Tel: 5-265293

Conference Connection

PO Box 12
York YO1 1YX
Tel 0904 643101

Dear Delegate,

Why not use the train for travelling to and from your conference? You will not be able to gain the most from your attendance if you are too tired to listen.

And nothing is more tiring than driving through bad weather, getting stuck in traffic jams and searching for a parking place.

Rail is fast, safe and comfortable. In most cases you can obtain a meal or refreshments as you travel. Alternatively you can sleep or work as you speed to your destination. And these benefits will not cost a lot. Included in this leaflet are special fares for conference delegates and you can take advantage of these provided you are staying overnight in the conference town.

To obtain your ticket complete the application form and send it, with your remittance, to the address shown. To allow time for processing please send your request as early as possible to reach us no less than 14 days in advance.

In a few instances, due to our zonal charging system, a cheaper fare could be available - please enquire at your nearest British Rail enquiry office whose telephone number can be found in the BT telephone directory.

Go by train - have a good conference.

Conference Officer

Read the letter from *Conference Connection* and then put a tick (✓) beside the right answers.

11 What does the letter say about food when travelling by train?

    A   Meals are available if ordered in advance. ....
    B   Refreshments are available on all trains. ....
    C   You can usually get something to eat and drink. ....
    D   You should take a packed meal with you. ....

12 If you want a special conference ticket you must

    A   telephone the Conference Officer in York. ....
    B   write to the Conference Officer at your local British Rail station. ....
    C   apply at a British Rail enquiry office. ....
    D   apply on a special application form. ....

13 If you want a conference ticket you should

    A   apply one week before your journey. ....
    B   apply at least two weeks before you travel. ....
    C   apply the day before you need it. ....
    D   apply more than four weeks before departure. ....

14 If you are applying for a conference ticket you must

    A   travel overnight to your conference town. ....
    B   book a seat in advance. ....
    C   travel in a group. ....
    D   spend a night in your conference town. ....

Focus on writing

FOOD, GLORIOUS FOOD

A survey of people's eating habits has shown that half the adults interviewed said they ate only one 'proper' meal a day. Two thirds of them said they ate four or more snacks during the day. On average, three-quarters of all eating occasions are classed as snacks.

One-third of adults (and as many as two-thirds of young single people) claim to eat a take-away meal at least once a week.

The most popular snacks are sandwiches, bread and butter or margarine, cake, confectionery, soft drinks, cheese, fruit and biscuits.

Source: MRB for The British Nutrition Foundation

1   You have been asked to write a short report for a student newspaper on eating habits in your country. Write about 100 words and mention what people eat and when they have their meals.

....

....

....

2   This is a picture of the traffic accident which you were involved in. You were the driver of the car. Write a letter to your insurance company explaining what happened. Use about 75 words. The letter has been started for you. Don't forget to put your address and the date on it.

Crossmills Insurance Company,
21 High Street,
Reading,
Berkshire.
RG1 2XA

Dear Sirs,
I am sending you my completed insurance claim form following an accident

which I was involved in last Friday. I was ....

....

....

Focus on listening

1 Listen to Penny and her friend Mark discussing their summer holiday plans
   and fill in the grid below with one word or short answers.

	PENNY'S CHOICE	MARK'S CHOICE	TOGETHER AGREE
COUNTRY			
TRANSPORT			
MONTH			
ACCOMMODATION			

2 Listen to Jane's phone call to her friend Sarah and then put a tick (✓) under the map
   which best describes where Jane is.

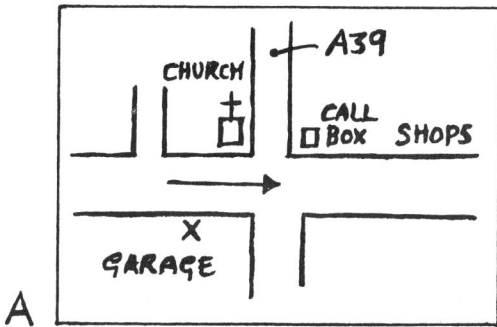

A

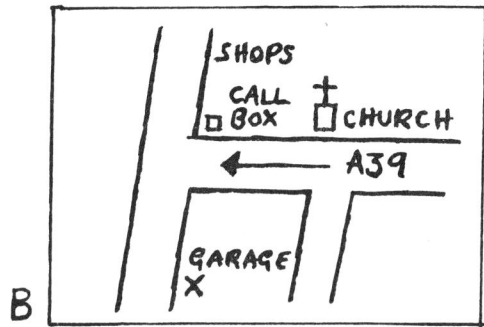

B

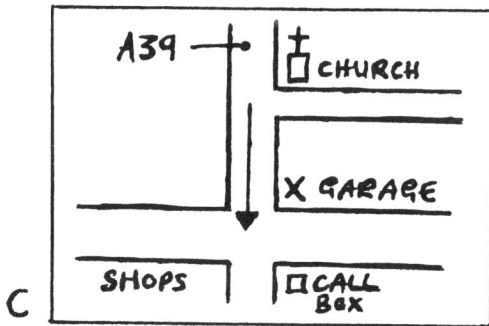

C

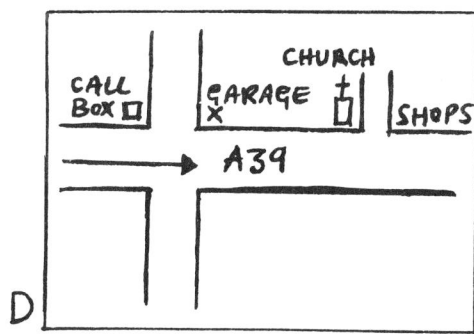

D

Level 2 Test 3

Focus on vocabulary

Underline the word that best completes each sentence.

e.g. The policeman .... the motorist for driving too fast.

   A told   B held   C <u>stopped</u>   D found

1   The price of land in central London is .... up all the time.

      A doing   B making   C letting   D going

2   My flat was .... into while I was away and my TV and video were stolen.

      A taken   B broken   C thrown   D gone

3   The teacher .... the children go home early because of the bad weather.

      A told   B allowed   C enabled   D let

4   The best .... about my new job is the extra money.

      A thing   B object   C idea   D stuff

5   When I was a child I wanted to be an actress but I changed my .... later on.

      A head   B heart   C mind   D memory

6   What advice would you .... someone who wanted to work in your country?

      A get   B give   C tell   D say

7   The car .... up sharply and two men jumped out.

      A pushed   B raised   C stepped   D pulled

8   Her .... is so quiet that you can hardly hear what she says.

      A noise   B voice   C sound   D way

9   When we are enjoying ourselves time .... by very quickly.

      A goes   B does   C moves   D runs

10   Anna decided to .... up with John when she met Richard.

      A make   B reach   C break   D hang

Focus on grammar

Use words in the list to complete the sentences.

over   down   after   out   from   into   of

1 I never like starting a new book, but once I get .... it it's all right.

2 I live about twenty miles .... Bristol.

3 Hold .... your hand and I'll read your life lines!

4 Half way .... the street I remembered I'd left my purse at home.

5 Could you buy me a box .... matches when you're out, please.

6 When are you going to Italy?

The day .... tomorrow.

7 I spent .... an hour trying to get my car to start this morning.

8 There is a university in Timbuctoo which dates .... around 1400.

9 Andrew did a lot .... damage when he backed .... his friend's car.

10 Look at this picture. The woman on the right has just found that her purse is missing. Write two more things that could have happened to the purse.

She could have dropped it among her shopping in her trolley.
She might have lost it while she was shopping.
She might have forgotten to bring it with her.
She may have left it in the bus or car.
Someone might have taken it while she wasn't looking.

....

....

Put a line under the correct word.

11 I know you .... me to be on time but the bus was late.   (said/told)

12 Did you .... twenty-two or thirty-two?   (tell/say)

13 If you don't know the price .... one of the shop assistants.   (ask/say)

14 Mary .... her husband she would be home by nine.   (asked/told)

15 I was in the middle of .... my daughter a story when the phone rang.   (telling/asking)

Complete the sentences by rearranging the words.

16 I think ....

books   it's   the   written   best   of   ever   one

17 The policeman said ....

tyres   wanted   my   that   to   he   check   car

18 She suddenly realised ....

been   her   had   handbag   stolen

Complete the second sentence so that it has the same meaning as the first.

19 The weather was cold but bright.

Although ....

20 He was an old man but that didn't stop him from walking ten miles a day.

Despite ....

The sentences below express   probability (certainty)   C
                               possibility (uncertainty)   U

Write C or U beside each sentence.

21 I wonder what could have happened to upset her.   ....

22 I must have left the front door open and that's how the burglar got in.   ....

23 There may be a storm tonight if the forecast is right.   ....

24 If you're lucky you might win something.   ....

25 No-one else was in here, so it must be you who took that money.   ....

Focus on reading

Read the information on 'Winter Festivals'* and then answer questions **1 – 6**.
Put a tick (✓) next to each statement if you think it is correct.

1   This information is written especially for children.   ....

2   The information covers four months of the year.   ....

3   There are three important events in November.   ....

4   'First Footing' takes place only in two countries.   ....

5   If you want good luck on New Year's Day you must invite a dark-haired

woman into your house.   ....

6   'Wassail' is an indoors festival.   ....

* A festival is a special day when people celebrate something which happened in the past.

❅ WINTER FESTIVALS ❅

The winter calendar for feasts and festivals is a busy one. There are religious holidays that recall important historical events; and the most important night of the year for witches and wizards!

Here are a few for you to celebrate this year:

Trafalgar Day : 21 October

In 1805 Horatio Nelson defeated the French and Spanish fleets at the battle of Trafalgar - probably the greatest Brisitsh victory at sea. This battle destroyed Napoleon's navy and brought Britain the command of the seas for a century.
Paxton's Tower, Dyfed was built by Sir William Paxton, a wealthy banker, as a tribute to Nelson. Nelson himself visited the Naval Temple at **The Kymin, Gwent** and was very impressed by what he called 'the only monument of the kind erected to the English Navy in the whole Kingdom'.

Bonfire Night : 5 November

A plan to blow up James and his Parliament was launched by a fanatical Catholic, Robert Catesby. The Gunpowder Plot, planned for 5 November 1605, was discovered and Guy Fawkes, the man who was to have lit the match, was executed along with all the other conspirators.

St Andrew's Day : 30 November

St Andrew was one of the twelve apostles and is the patron saint of Scotland. In Rumania vampires were

said to rise from their graves on St Andrew's Eve and haunt the houses where they used to live.

New Year's Eve : 31 December

This is the eve when we turn our back on the past and start afresh in the coming year. In Scotland and the north of England 'First Footing' is a very important part of New Year's Day. The first person to set foot in the house after midnight strikes and the old year ends, brings good or bad luck to the house. Any woman brings bad luck! If possible, the 'first footer' should be a stranger with dark hair bearing the gifts of a piece of coal, bread and some money or salt, to ensure warmth, food and wealth for the family throughout the year.

Twelth Night Epiphany : 6 January

As well as being Old Christmas Day (look at 'What do you know about Christmas' to find out more about this festival), and the last day of Christmas, this is also the day when it was customary to 'Wassail' the apple trees in the orchard.
The word 'wassail' comes from 'wes hal' meaning 'be of good health'. The farmer and his family , and the labourers and their families gathered around the best apple tree in the orchard after dusk. Shotguns were fired through the branches to raise the sleeping spirit and drive away the demons of bad luck. A little wassail or cider was then poured around the roots and a piece of toast, dipped in the wassail was wedged in the branches. Everyone sang the Wassail song, asking the trees to bear heavy crops of big apples.

Read the texts A, B, C and D.

7 Which text gives advice about preventing accidents? ....

8 Which text tells you how to slow down? ....

9 Which text are we meant to find funny? ....

10 Which text are we meant to find strange? ....

A The triangle of sea in the Atlantic Ocean that stretches from Bermuda to Puerto Rico to Miami is known as the Bermuda Triangle. Over the years, countless ships and aircraft are said to have disappeared in this area and no one appears to have any solution to the mystery. Aeroplanes have simply vanished from radar screens, ships have set out to sea and never returned. No sign of any wreckage has ever been found.

B

- Use your eyes
- Slow down
- Keep your distance

BE SAFETY-CONSCIOUS – STAY ALIVE

C In the interest of safety police wishing to stop a vehicle will do so, where possible, from behind.

They will attract your attention by flashing headlamps or the blue light, and/or sound the siren.

A police officer will indicate to you that you should pull over to the left, by pointing and showing the left side indicator. As soon as you can do so safely, pull over to the left and stop.

D I've been a serious jogger for about a year, and as I was warming up for a race I saw a man doing a stretching exercise. He was sitting in his parked car with one leg inside and his other foot on the ground outside the car. I watched as he bent his head down until it almost touched the ground and then held it there. I walked over to my car and tried the same thing. As I bent downwards, I could feel new muscles stretching and complimented myself on this discovery. Then I heard the man yell to his wife, 'Hey, darling, I've found the keys! They were under the car after all.'

11 Find words or phrases in the text below which mean:

take quickly ....

beginnings ....

very bad ....

almost no-one ....

In the same way ....

a short moment ....

'Bless you!'
It is the custom in Britain to say 'Bless you' when someone sneezes. It is said that this has its origin in the old belief that when someone sneezed their soul left their body for an instant. If the devil or some evil spirit happened to be about it would snatch the soul and carry it off. For this reason people said 'Bless you' to protect the sneezer against evil. Even though hardly anybody still believes this many people still say 'Bless you'.
Similarly people often say 'Touch wood' and touch some wooden object to bring luck. If you ask someone how they have done in an examination, for example, they might say 'Oh, quite well, I think. Touch wood'. The origin of this is not known.

12 Find phrases in the text below which mean:

see ....

not at all safe ....

more than one ....

say they won't ....

someone from the army on the opposite side (not a friend) ....

In the 1914-1918 war it was very dangerous to light a number of cigarettes from one match, especially at night-time. An enemy sharpshooter might catch sight of the match lighting the first cigarette; the second would give him time to take aim, and he would fire at the third. Because of this some people still refuse to light three cigarettes from one match.

Focus on writing

1   There has been a rise in crime in the area where you live. You and your friends are going to write an advice page for your local newspaper. Use the picture to help you. Write about 80 words.

2   Some friends are going to visit your country. You have been asked to suggest a hotel where they can stay. Use the texts to help you decide what to say if you wish. Write about 80 words.

Hotel Cottage

Modern hotel within easy reach of town centre (bus every 10 minutes stops outside hotel). Lounge, bar, noted restaurant and a splendid atrium garden. Swimming pool with snack bar and sauna. Bedrooms have bath and/or shower, radio, TV.

Hotel Wilson

Centrally situated on the Diagonal Avenue. Comfortable accommodation in the "chic" area. Air-conditioned bedrooms with colour TV, bath, shower and w.c. First floor lounge/bar.

Hotel City

Small, pleasant hotel on a quiet street directly above town and close to the city centre. Cafeteria-style restaurant, snack bar, laundry facilities, travel desk, bank and lift. Rooms with shower and w.c., radio and TV. Excellent value.

Focus on listening

Listen to recordings **1 – 4** and put a tick (✓) beneath the correct picture for each one.

1

   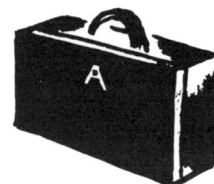

a ☐   b ☐   c ☐   d ☐

2

a ☐   b ☐   c ☐   d ☐

3

a ☐   b ☐   c ☐   d ☐

4

a ☐   b ☐   c ☐   d ☐

5 Mr and Mrs Hewlett's house has been burgled. Listen to Mr Hewlett telling the police officer about it and fill in the blanks in the police officer's notebook.

> 21/7/89
> 18 Thornton Rd Mr + Mrs Hewlett
> Burglary-Stolen property:
> – gold . . . .
> – . . . . cash
> – cheque book
> . . . . cheques left
>   worth about £600
> Burglars got in through . . . .
> – – – – – – – – – – – – – – – –
> Smashed lock. Ask security officer to advise.

Level 3 Test 1

Focus on vocabulary

Complete sentences **1 – 10** by forming a new word from the word given in capitals.

E.g. The criminal could offer no *explanation* .... for his actions.   EXPLAIN

1   My father died less than two years after his ....   RETIRE

2   Lucy has such a lovely .... that it's not surprising she's so popular.   PERSON

3   I intend writing a letter of .... to my local council.   COMPLAIN

4   The .... to the book was very interesting.   INTRODUCE

5   The design for the new theatre is really exciting and ....   IMAGINE

6   Maria has applied for the job of .... at the new supermarket.   MANAGE

7   The best place to watch the birds is from the .... hut.   OBSERVE

8   He reads widely and consequently has an excellent general............................. .   KNOW

9   Harry gets a lot of .... from playing the piano.   SATISFY

10   Mrs. Travis has accepted the post of hospital............................. .   ADMINISTER

Complete sentences **11 – 15** by adding one of the following words:

violent   smoking   existent   stop   alcoholic

11   Only non-........................ drinks were served at the school disco.

12   Most cinemas in the UK now provide a non-........................ seating area.

13   If you fly non-.................... from England to Hong Kong you can do the journey in under 15 hours.

14   The bus service in some parts of rural Wales is non-........................ .

15   The police allowed the student protest to continue provided it remained non-.................... .

Focus on grammar

Fill the gaps using **a**, **an** or **the** or leave a space if you think nothing is required.

HOLIDAY HEALTH CHECKLIST

①　Have..........small first aid kit with you.

②　Sterilise your drinking water; you can do this by boiling
　　..........water or using sterilisation tablets.

③　Never eat..........meat or fish which is not properly cooked.

④　Avoid sitting in..........sun for too long.

⑤　If you are bitten by..........animal, go immediately
　　to..........nearest doctor or hospital.

Fill in the gaps with the correct form of one of the following verbs:

put　　take　　go　　do

6　I .... a week off work when my mother went into hospital so that I could look after the family.

7　At the end of the Drama Course a show was .... on for the public.

8　John .... his medical training in Manchester.

9　Sarah worked abroad for five years, then .... home to Australia.

10　It has .... many years for people to realise the dangers of smoking.

Underline the most suitable verb.

11　When I was a child I ... (used to/could) have dancing lessons. Every

12　week my mother .... (would/had to) take me to a large old house where

13　I ... (had to/would) join a group of children who all seemed as bored as me!

14　We ... (used to/could) spend hours walking and skipping around the room while

15　some elderly man ... (would/had to) play the piano – very badly as I remember!

Use **do** or **don't** to complete the sentences.

16 Please .... wear indoor shoes in the gymnasium or you will damage

the floor.

17 .... worry if the fire alarm bell rings as there will be a fire drill practice

later on today.

18 I .... wish Dominic would tidy his bedroom!

19 I'm not very keen on Indian food, but I .... love Chinese!

20 .... please ask me any questions you like if you want to know more

about the history of this castle.

Complete the sentences using a suitable preposition e.g. **on**, **in** etc.

21 Katy blew .... all the candles on the cake in one go.

22 Mrs. Brown was knocked .... by a bus and later died in hospital.

23 The plane blew .... over the sea killing everyone on board.

24 When I was six I fell .... a wall and broke my arm.

Rewrite the following phrases using **noun + noun**.

Example: an article consisting of news .... *a news article* .

25 someone who is learning to drive ....

26 a party where people sit and have dinner together ....

27 the engine of a car ....

Complete the sentences.

28 When I was small I used to hate eating cabbage, whereas ....

....

29 Howard loves flying, unlike his sister who ....

30 Olivia doesn't eat meat and neither ....

31 Stephen has worked all over the world, unlike Hilary who ....

....

32 Whereas John is very good at sport, I ....

Focus on reading and dictionary skills

1   Read the text and then match each word or phrase in the left-hand column with
    one on the right.

St.Valentine's Day, February 14th, has been a customary day for choosing
sweethearts and exchanging love-tokens from time immemorial. Countless generations of young people have acknowledged St. Valentine as the
friend and patron of lovers.

The method of choosing sweethearts on St. Valentine's Day varied in
different times and places. It could be a serious matter, leading to
marriage, or it could be a kind of game. Sometimes pure chance was the
deciding factor. There was a common belief that the first man seen by
any woman on February 14th must be her Valentine, whether she liked
him or not. Great care was therefore needed to ensure that the first man
encountered was the right one. Some modern schoolgirls still believe this,
or pretend to do so, and have been known to go about with their eyes
closed until they know it is safe to open them!

customary	• •	an important event
choosing	• •	traditional
generation	• •	all right
method	• •	act as though they
varied	• •	something generally thought to be true
a serious matter	• •	picking
a common belief	• •	walk around
pretend to	• •	differed
go about	• •	people who have lived at different times
safe	• •	particular way

Read the text then answer questions **2 – 9** by putting a tick (✓) beside a statement if you think it is true.

I n 1779, Lord Thomas Lyttleton dreamt that he was to die in three days' time at midnight. It upset him so much that the following morning he told all his friends. They tried to reassure him that everything would be all right, but he could not get the dream out of his mind. During the following days he suffered bouts of extreme depression as the fatal hour neared.

On the third evening, he invited some guests to dinner in an attempt to forget about the dream. As midnight approached he became more and more depressed. Eventually he could take no more, and retired to his bedroom to await death.

He lay on his bed and watched the clock tick away his final seconds. As the clock struck midnight Lord Lyttleton wondered how he was to die – but nothing happened! A few minutes later one of his guests looked into the room to see how he was and was surprised to find the Lord in the highest of spirits. 'I've beaten death,' cried Lyttleton. 'I'll be down to join you all shortly.'

When the butler entered the room a little later, he found his lordship lying on the bed gasping for breath. The butler rushed downstairs for help, but it was too late. Lord Lyttleton was dead. 'Well,' said one of the guests, looking at the bedroom clock, 'his dream was almost right, but the time was slightly wrong. It's now half past twelve.'

'No, sir. It is not,' said the butler. 'Because his lordship was so worried, I took the liberty of altering all the household clocks earlier today.' The dream was true – Lyttleton died on the stroke of midnight.

---

2   Lord Lyttleton was not afraid of dying.

3   Lord Lyttleton had the same dream three times.

4   Lord Lyttleton's friends knew about his dream.

5   Lord Lyttleton felt very nervous around midday.

6   Lord Lyttleton's friend found him awake.

7   One of the guests had changed the time on the clocks.

8   Lord Lyttleton did not die alone.

9   Lord Lyttleton's dream came true.

butler /bʌtlə/, **butlers.** A **butler** is the most important male servant in a house.

Read the sentences below then match each word in **bold** type with its dictionary definition.

10   Mrs Brown found a painting in her attic which turned out to be an **original** Picasso.

11   The child woke up screaming in terror from her **nightmare**.

12   Don't **assume** that everyone shares your superstitious ideas.

13   Now that Mr Smith has retired he **seldom** goes out.

14   He spent two years **training** before he set out to climb Mount Everest.

1 If you ⊏ ⊐ that something is true, you imagine that it is true, sometimes wrongly. ᴇɢ *I* ⊏ ⊐ *you don't drive... I was mistakenly* ⊏ *to be a Welshman because of my surname.*

2 You refer to a work of art or a document as an ⊏ ⊐ when it is genuine and not a copy. ᴇɢ *The* ⊏ ⊐ *is in the British Museum.* ▸ used as an adjective. ᴇɢ *...working on* ⊏ ⊐ *documents.*

A ⊏ ⊐ is **1** a very frightening dream. ᴇɢ *He rushed to her room when she had* ⊏ ⊐ *and comforted her.*

6 If you ⊏ ⊐ for a sports match or a race, you prepare for it by doing exercises and eating a special diet.

. If something ⊏ ⊐ happens, it happens only occasionally. ᴇɢ *It* ⊏ ⊐ *rains there... The waiting time was* ⊏ ⊐ *less than four hours... He* ⊏ ⊐ *feels confident.*

Focus on writing

1   This is part of a story written by an eight year old girl. Rewrite the story and add the punctuation you would need to put in, if you were going to read it aloud.

> I was packing a few sandwiches and some drink all into my rucksack snow was falling steadily outside and the grass looked like icing on a cake the howling rain and wind nearly put us off but we still went out the moon rising over the pine trees made the whole scene look very romantic then when I looked up to the sky I saw lots of broken clouds one of them looked like a young girl another a man running and another a bird of prey swooping down

....

....

....

....

....

HOLIDAY GUIDES are required to accompany our holiday makers who will be spending part of their holiday tour in your town. Each tour lasts one week and the holidays operate from June to September. Applicants who speak a foreign language will have an advantage.
Full details of the programme will be sent on receipt of your application.

Write a letter applying for a job as a holiday guide in a town you know giving details of your education, experience and ability to do the job. Write about 100 words. Don't forget to date the letter and add your address.

The Manager,
Panorama Tours,
King's Square,
Chichester,
Sussex.

Dear Sir,

....

....

....

....

....

....

....

....

....

....

....

Focus on listening

1   Fill in the gaps in the notes the teacher makes as he talks to the students.

Student interviews
Oscar Father owns a
_____ business. Hopes
to study Economics
Business Management
at university Will
eventually work _____

_____

Linda Half Norwegian
half _____ studying
here because she _____

_____

says that Norwegians
like _____ Has a
sense of humour.

2   Listen to Ken talking to Philip about his holiday in Paris.

For questions **a – f** put a tick (✓) in the box if you agree with the statement.

a   Ken spent a week in Paris. ☐

b   Ken flew from London to Paris. ☐

c   Ken had been to Paris before. ☐

d   Ken is hoping to visit Paris again. ☐

e   Ken spent all the time in Paris. ☐

f   Ken travelled with a couple of friends. ☐

Level 3 Test 2

Focus on vocabulary

Fill the gaps with a suitable verb.

1 When you see David would you .... him a message from me, please?

2 Professor Bluff is a clever man but he finds it difficult to .... his ideas across in his lectures.

3 Bianca is very good at .... advice but not so good at taking it!

4 Could you explain to me again what you mean – I didn't .... it the first time.

5 The motorway crash .... up the traffic for almost two hours.

6 Match the pairs.

good	• •	tragedy
harmless	• •	friend
death	• •	tight
enemy	• •	deadly
comedy	• •	birth
loose	• •	evil

For **7 - 16** the word in capitals at the end of each sentence can be used to form a new word that fits in the blank space.

7 You haven't .... this parcel properly – it'll come undone in the post.   TIE

8 My mother was one of the best .... of her generation.   ACT

9 I'd like to meet around ten o'clock, but if that's .... perhaps you're free later on the same day.   CONVENIENT

10 After the Second World War many European refugees living in Britain applied for British ....   NATION

11 John's .... outbursts often lead him to regret his actions.   PASSION

12 .... harmony is essential if different ethnic groups are to live together.   RACE

13 In the past few years .... has become an increasingly important subject.   CONSERVE

14 She was so exhausted by the climb she could .... speak.   SCARCE

15 Her numerous activities have earned her the reputation of being a most professional ....   CAMPAIGN

16 The law governing child safety belts in cars becomes .... later this year.   EFFECT

© Collins ELT, 1989
COBUILD is a trademark of William Collins Sons and Company Limited

Focus on grammar

Complete the following with a suitable phrase.

1   The worrying thing .... the number of plane crashes appears to be increasing.

2   It's .... drive too fast in case you have an accident.

3   It's .... have friends especially when you're in need of help.

4   The trouble with John .... he never stops talking!

5   If you lose your passport when you're abroad the best thing would be ....

    ....

Fill in the gaps using **whose**, **which** or **where**.

6   The coat .... Anne borrowed from her sister was far too big for her.

7   Dominic, ... interest in space travel began when he was a child, last week became

    the first British astronaut in space.

8   Most of the passengers in the rail crash managed to escape through the window ....

    had been shattered.

9   You must keep this camera in a place .... it won't get damaged.

10 The man .... house was broken into was himself a burglar!

Fill in each space with one word.

11 The .... I read about West Africa the .... I should like to go there as

    it sounds so interesting.

12 The bigger the sum of money collected the .... !

13 The .... I study Russian the easier it becomes.

14 The .... we destroy our environment the safer it will be for the next generation.

15 The .... I have to deal with rude children the .... I like being a teacher.

Rewrite the second sentence so that it means the same as the first.

16 Although the train was late I still arrived at the meeting on time.

Despite ....

17 Even though it rained the football match was not cancelled.

The football match was not cancelled despite ....

18 What a pity I can't drive.

I wish ....

19 What a pity I got married.

I wish ....

20 Jim sold his car to the garage for £1000.

The garage ....

Complete these sentences using an appropriate verb form.

21 I would have gone to university if ....

22 You .... seen Mary in town yesterday because she's out of the country.

23 If you don't feel well you .... see a doctor.

24 If you had asked me earlier I .... able to help you.

25 I don't know whether I've passed the exam – it was very difficult so I .... failed.

Underline the correct question tag.

26 It looks as if it's going to rain, (isn't it/doesn't it)?

27 Your name wouldn't be Richard (would it/can it)?

28 It was Sam who borrowed my bike, (mustn't it/wasn't it)?

29 Sally has grown up a lot recently, (doesn't she/hasn't she)?

30 This must be the last question, (mustn't it/isn't it)?

Focus on reading and dictionary skills

Fill in each gap with one word only.

Third Boeing air disaster

144 die in Azores tragedy

THE giant plane maker Boeing is trying to work out what went wrong after yet another of its jets fell ①.......... of the sky.

Experts are still studying wreckage from ②.......... Boeing 707 that crashed last week in the Azores. The first inspection suggested that either the plane had gone wrong ③.......... the pilot had made ④.......... mistake, but it seemed unlikely ⑤.......... bomb had caused the disaster.

Rescuers reached the scene quickly, ⑥.......... there were no survivors out of the 144 people on board.

Read the text and then answer **7 – 11** by putting a tick (✓) in the box if you think the statement is correct.

Rat army takes over sewers

A PLAGUE of rats is rapidly taking over the system of underground pipes that make up Britain's sewers, according to the people who run our biggest cities.

They have reported an alarming increase in the number of disease-carrying rodents in cities stretching from Newcastle and Wakefield in the north, to London in the south.

What's worse – the rats have started to creep out of the sewers, claims a report by the Association of Metropolitan Authorities. The association carried out a survey throughout last year and found that twice as many rats were spotted in some parts of the country as the year before.

The water authorities are responsible for keeping the pest under control. They not only supply fresh water, but also deal with the waste that goes through the sewers. And rats have been occupying the thoughts of Princess Anne too. She was due to visit a rat infested camp of gypsies, or travellers, in Wales last week.

Normally people try to smarten up their homes when a member of the royal family visit. But when they heard the Princess Royal was coming to see them, the gypsies were determined that she should see how bad their living conditions are.

7 There are more rats in Britain's cities than there used to be. ☐

8 The rats live in old houses. ☐

9 It is the duty of the water authorities to deal with the rats. ☐

10 There are rats in the gypsy camp. ☐

11 The gypsies cleaned up the camp for their royal visitor. ☐

Read the article *Jungle Troubles* and answer questions **12 – 15** by putting
a tick (✓) against the ending which best completes each sentence.

JUNGLE TROUBLES

BY THE time you finish reading this article 500 acres of Tropical Rainforests will have been destroyed and yet another species will be on its way to extinction.

Already this century people have destroyed around half of the world's rainforests and the threat to the remaining half has become so serious that saving it has become top priority for the conservation group, World Wide Fund for Nature (WWF).

Much of the forest has been destroyed because of people looking for more land to graze cattle, chopping down trees to sell commercially as timber and mineral mining.

FOREST DEVASTATION

Once large amounts have been cut down the plants cannot grow quickly enough to replace the felled forest.

The hard and heavy tropical rains which make the forest so lush soon wash away the topsoil on the bare ground and make it impossible to use any more.

It is not only plants and trees that are being destroyed but also the many thousands of animal species which live within the forest. Beautiful animals like the jaguar and orang-utang are under serious threat as well as many thousands of smaller animals, many of which will never be discovered before they die out.

And the plants of the rainforest do not just act as shelter for the animals and many human tribes that live off the rainforest. Some have valuable medicinal qualities.

MEDICINAL QUALITIES

The rosy periwinkle for example, has been found to have properties which help to cure child leukaemia. Since the discovery a child suffering from the disease has an 80 per cent chance of survival, before it was only 20 per cent.

Many conservation groups like Friends of the Earth are setting up projects to try and save the diminishing rainforests.

WWF has begun an ambitious project to help protect the Korup rainforest in Cameroon, West Africa which shelters a quarter of all the monkey species found on the continent.

The rugged terrain of the Korup makes it useless for agriculture and there are no valuable mineral reserves inside the forest. It is still threatened with destruction because of hunters.

The hunters go into the forest with their modern weapons to kill animals like the leopard and elephant and many others.

But the Korup forest depends upon its animals and birds to pollinate plants and protect the delicate balance of its ecosystem.

With the help of WWF the Cameroon government made Korup into a national park in 1982. They hope to make the park sustain itself and also benefit the Korup people.

Already they have started tree nurseries that will supply the locals with fast-growing timber to prevent excessive forest destruction.

WWF experts are working with Cameroon scientists to discover how they can use the benefits of the forest without destroying it.

Support for projects like this and others similar are vital to the survival of the rainforests.

Even here in Britain we can stop adding to the destruction of the forest by avoiding buying tropical hardwood. Friends of the Earth have a list of all woods which come from the rainforest called the Good Wood Guide.

If you would like to know more about the rainforest and find out how you can help contact Godalming Surrey GU7 1BR Tel : 0483 426444.

12   The purpose of this article is to

- encourage people to holiday in West Africa.   A ☐
- advertise the attractions of game parks.   B ☐
- explain what is happening to rainforests.   C ☐
- persuade people to visit rainforests.   D ☐

13   Tropical plants are an important source of

- food.   A ☐
- fuel.   B ☐
- medicine.   C ☐
- minerals.   D ☐

14   The Korup is valuable for its

- monkeys.   A ☐
- agriculture.   B ☐
- minerals.   C ☐
- trees.   D ☐

15   Friends of the Earth want people to

- give money towards protecting wild animals.   A ☐
- send money direct to the Cameroon Government.   B ☐
- help in selling tropical hardwood products.   C ☐
- refuse to buy products made from certain trees.   D ☐   ☐

Focus on writing

1   Write down three pieces of advice you would want to give someone thinking of visiting your country for the first time.

a   ....

    ....

    ....

b   ....

    ....

    ....

c   ....

    ....

    ....

2   Write a short story based on the picture strip below. Use about 100 words.

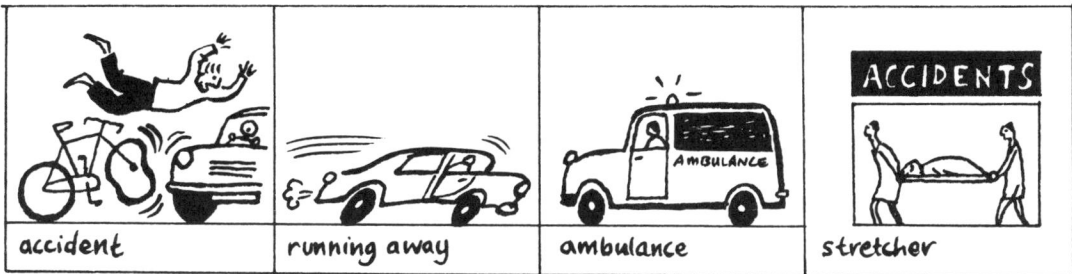

| accident | running away | ambulance | stretcher |

....

....

....

....

....

....

....

....

....

....

Focus on listening

Listen to Dot talking about what went wrong on her journey to Gatwick airport, not far from London. She also mentions Heathrow airport which is close to London. For questions **1 – 12** put a tick (✔) in the box beside each statement if you think it is true.

1	Dot says her journey was the worst thing that had ever happened to her.	☐
2	The train was delayed for thirty minutes.	☐
3	Dot was told she would miss the connecting train.	☐
4	The station master was very helpful.	☐
5	Dot was advised to catch a bus to Heathrow.	☐
6	When Dot found the bus to Gatwick had left she began to cry.	☐
7	Dot did not have enough money for the taxi fare.	☐
8	The taxi driver asked for a cheque.	☐
9	The taxi driver suggested that Dot should give him her watch.	☐
10	Dot's husband needed the taxi driver's name and address.	☐
11	The taxi driver followed Dot into the airport.	☐
12	The Norwegian told Dot a joke when she arrived.	☐

Level 3 Test 3

Focus on vocabulary

For questions **1 – 12** use the word in capitals at the end of each sentence to form a word that fits in each space.

1   After careful .... Fiona decided to accept the offer of a job abroad.   CONSIDER

2   The knowledge that he had never lost a tennis match gave him a definite ....

    advantage over his opponents.   PSYCHOLOGY

3   The teacher warned the class that it was their .... to make sure that they

    handed in their work on time.   RESPONSIBLE

4   What started off as a minor disagreement .... developed into a full-scale

    argument.   RAPID

5   Recent .... in relations between East and West have led to fresh hopes for

    peace.   DEVELOP

6   Some of the .... at the conference walked out in anger after hearing the

    Minister's speech.   REPRESENT

7   Living overseas gives foreign correspondents the opportunity to understand the ....

    background of a country.   CULTURE

8   The police arrested twenty .... during the anti-nuclear march.   PROTEST

9   There was a .... of fresh vegetables after the long hard winter.   SHORT

10   Emily is a very .... girl and you can always trust her to keep her word.   RELY

11   If you want to become a .... you have to be prepared to work very long hours.

    POLITICS

12   The bombs dropped during the Second World War caused a great deal of ....

    in some parts of Europe.   DESTROY

Focus on grammar

Complete the sentences by writing the correct preposition.

1   This is the box .... which the burglar hid the money.

2   Which country do you come .... ?

3   Tom was told to be home by ten, instead .... which he arrived after midnight.

4   I've got a brochure we can choose our package holiday ....

5   Which university are you hoping to go .... ?

Rewrite each sentence so that it means exactly the same as the original.

6   One cheap way of seeing the world is to hitch-hike.

   One cheap way to ....

7   Once David had lost his job he gave up the idea of getting married.

   Once David had lost his job he gave up the idea that ....

8   The train journey from London to Aberdeen takes nine hours.

   It's a ....

9   Had you asked my permission before borrowing my car I would not have been so angry.

   If ....

   ....

10   I would have gone to the cinema with you if I'd known you were going.

   Had ....

   ....

Complete the following sentences with an appropriate ending.

E.g. Delighted by his examination success, Rick *gave a party* ....
for all his friends.

11 Concerned about the rise in crime, the government ....

....

12 Given the opportunity to study abroad, I would ....

....

13 Interviewed on the TV news, the President ....

....

14 Encouraged by her teachers to become a journalist, Diane ....

....

15 Adopted by a large fun-loving family when he was only six weeks old, Sam ....

....

Fill in the gaps in the following table.

	NOUN	VERB	ADJECTIVE
16	dependence	depend	....
17	competition	....	competing
18	....	level	level
19	proposal	propose	....
20	....	equalise	equal

Fill in each gap with one word.

21 I don't know .... to thank you enough for all the help you've given me.

22 I don't know .... to go for my holiday this year.

23 When the fire alarm bell rang no one had any idea .... to do.

24 I like both these books so much, I really don't know .... one to buy.

25 I know so few people it's hard to know .... to turn to for advice.

Focus on reading and dictionary skills

Match each of the headlines below with its accompanying text.

1

HEROISM AS PILOT SAVES SCHOOL

A An Austrian skier was killed when he strayed off piste in the Italian Alps yesterday.

2

MUCH TOO CHEAP AT THE PRICE

B The number of foreigners studying at British universities and polytechnics has recovered to the number it was at before the decision to charge full-cost fees.

3

IT'S OFFICIAL: GIRLS ARE TOUGHER THAN BOYS

C Cindy is 13 and has had a weekend job on a market stall since she was ten. She is paid £5 for 22 hours and only has a break of one hour in each 11-hour day.

4

AVALANCHE DEATH

D Pupils cheated death when a helicopter crashed and blew up in a courtyard of their school in Spain.

5

NUMBER OF FOREIGN STUDENTS UP AGAIN

E Don't look so shocked. It's all true. All over the prosperous, industrial world, females' life expectancy is years greater than males.

Headline 1 goes with ....

Headline 2 goes with ....

Headline 3 goes with ....

Headline 4 goes with ....

Headline 5 goes with ....

6   Rearrange the following paragraphs to form the original newspaper article.

A
"No one need ever know that these are the children of lepers, and that's important", I'm told, as I watch them, immaculately turned out in their maroon and white uniforms, repeating the Nepalese alphabet parrot-fashion. In a country where male literacy is estimated at 33 per cent and female only 5 per cent, these are privileged children.

B
The camp has been here for 140 years and, according to the Adventist Development and Relief Agency, which assumed administrative control of the colony two years ago, is the only remaining leper colony in the world.

C
Until ADRA arrived, the school at the camp was open only 10 days a year. It now provides a decent primary education to the youngsters before they progress to secondary schooling in Kathmandu.

D
Ten miles from Kathmandu, bustling capital of Nepal and infamous hangout of the 1960s hippy and 1980s trekker, is the Khokana leper colony. Nestling in the foothills of the Himalayas, in a green and fertile valley, is the home of some 2,000 lepers and their children.

E
An adult education class is also getting under way, lepers with only stumps for hands somehow manage to clasp a pencil and write legibly. A teacher from Kathmandu visits twice a week. A training centre for skills development will start soon, producing shoes and carpets and such like, to bring in a little outside income.

leprosy /lɛprəsi¹/ is a serious infectious disease that damages people's skin and flesh.

The right order is ....

Read statements **7 – 10**, then check to see whether they are true by examining the graphs and diagrams and reading the article. Then put a tick (✔) in the box if you agree with the statement.

7   More women than men use bank credit cards.   ☐

8   Over twenty-two million people use credit cards.   ☐

9   Thirteen per-cent of purchases are made using plastic money.   ☐

10   More than half a million people have a Marks and Spencer credit card.   ☐

A quarter of a century ago plastic cards were introduced as a means of paying for goods and service by credit.

Credit cards now account for something like 13 per cent of non-cash transactions in Great Britain but they still generate paper in the form of credit card vouchers and cheques to be processed through the banking system.

Paper is expensive to process which is why credit card issuers are extending the role of the plastic card to enable customers to make electronic transactions directly with their accounts.

By adding a magnetic strip encoded with the account number and other details, the card becomes the key to a computer terminal and can be used for drawing on bank accounts or extending customer's credit.

UK banks offer several cards performing various services and more and more stores are now issuing their own cards. In April this year Marks and Spencer introduced a retail credit card for their customers and to date nearly 750,000 accounts have been opened and more than one million cards issued (an increase in the total number of store cards which is not reflected in the accompanying tables).

At present cards are used to draw cash, guarantee cheques and pay for goods and services by credit. However, there is already some experimentation with cards which permit the transfer of payment electronically at the point of sale. Instant, rather than deferred payment by credit card may be the face of the future.

How many cards are there?

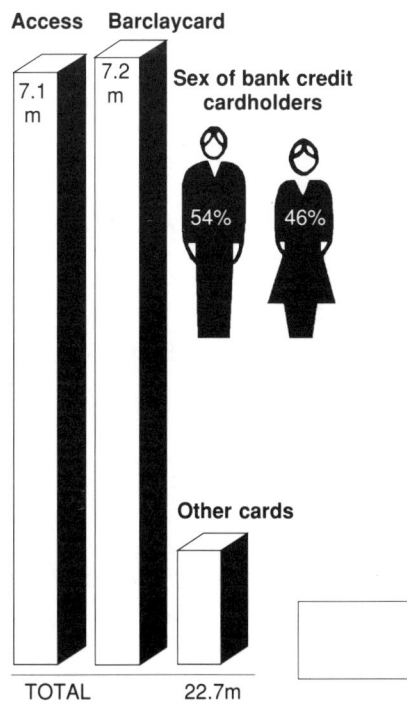

Access   Barclaycard

7.1 m   7.2 m

Sex of bank credit cardholders

54%   46%

Other cards

TOTAL   22.7m

Put a line under the odd word out in each set.

11 troops   soldiers   army   farmer   guards

12 overthrow   broadcast   win   lose   defeat

Look at the definition and example and underline the correct word from the following list that goes with the definition.

13 lose   act   fall   cut   strike

2 If you ⊏ ⊐ a close relative or friend, he or she dies. EG I ⊏ ⊐ my father when I was nine.

14 soft   thick   old   dumb   dim

2 If your memory of something is ⊏ ⊐ you can hardly remember it at all. EG I only have a ⊏ ⊐ recollection of the production.

Focus on writing

1 Make all the necessary changes and additions to the following sets of words in order to produce a complete letter.

EXAMPLE: I/very pleased/present/you send/me/my birthday yesterday.

I was very pleased with the present you sent me for my birthday yesterday.

21 The Liberty
Wells.
March 9th 1989

Dear Sir,

I write/complain/packet/biscuits/I buy/your store last week.

....

When I open/packet/I find/piece metal inside.

....

Be fortunate/I not/swallow it.

....

I enclose/piece metal/together/receipt/biscuits.

....

I look forward/hear/you/soon possible.

....

Yours faithfully,

H.C. Foulkes.

2 The charts below show where British people have taken their holidays in 1987 and 1988. Use the information to write a short report for a popular newspaper. Write about 80 words.

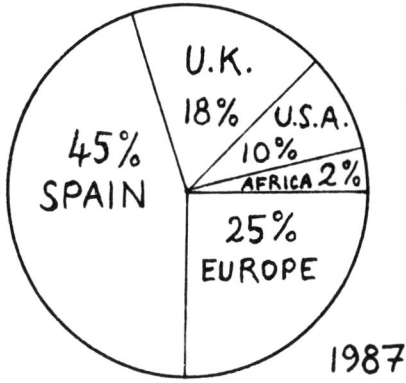

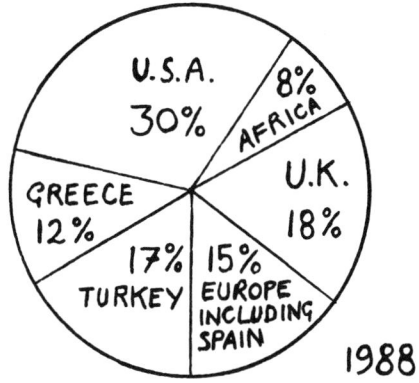

1987 pie chart: 45% SPAIN, U.K. 18%, U.S.A. 10%, AFRICA 2%, 25% EUROPE

1988 pie chart: U.S.A. 30%, 8% AFRICA, U.K. 18%, 15% EUROPE INCLUDING SPAIN, 17% TURKEY, GREECE 12%

....

....

....

....

....

....

....

....

Write an introductory paragraph (between 30-40 words) for each of the following headlines.

3

ANOTHER RAIL CRASH

....

....

....

....

....

....

4

SOLDIER DROWNS

....

....

....

....

....

Focus on listening

Listen to Gill Windlesham talking about her work with the British Council. For questions **1 – 12** fill in the information on the notepad with either one word or short phrases.

Gillian Windlesham — Specialist tourist

is a ① _____ writer but

② _____ works for British Council

Gives lectures, seminars, courses etc.

Usually knows about trip③ _____ in advance

Finds residential courses interesting

Doesn't like giving ④ _____ because

⑤ _____

Has visited many countries; next trip will

be ⑥ _____

Preparation for a trip involves

either writing or ⑦ _____ people

May have to order ⑧ _____ and⑨ _____

recognised at airports by ⑩ _____

Highlights: riding on a sledge in Poland

going to first night at the ⑪ _____

⑫ _____ in Hong Kong

Level 3 Test 4

Focus on vocabulary

For questions **1 – 20** choose the word or phrase which best completes each
sentence by putting a circle around the letter A, B, C, or D.

E.g. The policeman .... the thief's arm as he tried to run away.

   A urged   B pushed   Ⓒ grabbed   D fixed

1 The terrorist .... suicide by blowing himself up.

   A made   B achieved   C did   D committed

2 A lot of people believed the TV .... about spaghetti growing on trees,

forgetting that it was being shown on April 1st.

   A lie   B hoax   C experiment   D mystery

3 I agree with Victor's ideas .... but find them hard to put into practice.

   A in turn   B in secret   C in principle   D in sight

4 There is a .... hope that the men trapped underground may still be alive.

   A faint   B dim   C light   D weak

5 Most people can't .... to see young children being badly treated.

   A support   B stand   C undergo   D bear

6 The ship .... heavily during the storm.

   A moved   B rolled   C turned   D waved

7 The accident happened at a point where the road ....

   A changed   B fell   C dipped   D curled

8 The hijacker lay dying on the ship's deck in a .... of blood.

   A pool   B spot   C drop   D bath

9 She .... up behind his chair so that he didn't hear her coming.

   A marched   B ran   C crept   D slipped

10 He stared into .... without really seeing anything in particular.

   A distance   B space   C atmosphere   D room

11 Certain .... are stronger than others on the international market.

 A   monies   B   pounds   C   coins   D   currencies

12 If you .... for peace, prepare for war.

 A   like   B   want   C   wish   D   desire

13 Britain and France will eventually be .... by the Channel Tunnel.

 A   tied   B   linked   C   fastened   D   involved

14 Even though Julie's only six she's very .... for her age.

 A   sensible   B   sufficient   C   wide   D   safe

15 The BBC World Service broadcasts many current affairs ....

 A   news   B   summaries   C   programmes   D   commentaries

16 'I must have been .... to let you go abroad alone – I should have know

 I couldn't trust you', Kitty's father said crossly.

 A   out of the question B   called to mind   C   out of control   D   out of my mind

17 The .... look on his face told her that something was wrong.

 A   heavy   B   grave   C   strong   D   slow

18 My father's .... came from Czechoslovakia to settle in the States.

 A   founders   B   generations   C   ancestors   D   historians

19 My parents got .... when I was seven and never saw each other again.

 A   split   B   divorced   C   cut   D   divided

20 After spending most of his wage packet James didn't have much ....

 A   in addition   B   left out   C   on top   D   left over

Focus on grammar

Rewrite the following sentences putting the adverbs in the right place; each one has been partly done for you. (More than one position is often possible.)

1   glanced   small   at   the   boy   nervously   policeman   the   up

     The small boy ....

2   cancelled   last   the   trip   minute   was   unfortunately   at   the

     .... at the last minute.

3   room   she   the   unusually   entered   the   serious   looked   teacher   as

     The teacher looked ....

4   weather   was   of   it   rough   pretty   go   such   silly   sailing   you   to   in

     .... in such rough weather.

5   man   the   onto   carefully   they   bed   injured   lifted   the

     They ....

Complete each of the following with a suitable phrase.

6   If I won a lot of money ....

7   When my grandmother was a child her family were so poor that ....

     ....

8   Whenever I think of England ....

9   One day when I was ....

10   It is obvious that ....

Write a full sentence to explain what the phrases mean.

     E.g. A tennis court *is an area where you play a game of tennis.*

11   A family party ....

12   A lifebelt ....

13   Sports clothes ....

14   Border guards ....

15   A smoking room ....

Complete the sentences with a suitable conjunction.

16 All ships must carry lifeboats .... of emergencies.

17 The workers are planning to strike .... the management agrees to an

increase in wages.

18 I may be old .... I'm not stupid!

19 He can't learn to drive yet .... he's only fifteen.

20 .... she didn't feel well she insisted on going to the meeting.

Focus on reading and dictionary skills

Read the following passage and fill in each blank with one word only.

Reaching new heights of daring

TWO of the world's greatest adventurers have said they are planning an air journey more spectacular and dangerous than any ever attempted before.

What's more, if all goes well, (1).......... will only last four hours. They're going (2).......... fly over Mount Everest in a hot air balloon.

The plan is to take (3).......... at least 20 miles away from Mount Everest in Nepal and drift with (4).......... wind over the mountain and into the country of Tibet. No-one (5).......... ever done this before because, until now, the government of Tibet had always refused to give (6).......... .

The balloon, (7).......... Star Flyer, has been specially designed to reach 10,000 metres. At that (8).......... it will clear the (9).......... of the mountain by 1,000 metres.

The real danger is (10)........ unpredictable weather. If the wind (11)........ them in the (12)........ direction, they face almost certain death. They could crash land high in the Himalayas. Resue (13).......... be impossible; there are no roads (14).......... the area and helicopters can't operate in the thin air at those heights.

(15).......... the equipment will have to be carried across mountain trails to the landing site many miles (16).......... the nearest road. It will take days to get (17).........., the balloon (18).......... carried like a giant sausage by teams (19).......... porters.Then the crew will wait (20).......... the weather and wind is exactly right.

Read the leaflet 'Controlling Your Lifestyle', then answer questions 21 – 30 by putting a tick (✓) beside each statement depending on whether it is **true** or **false** according to the leaflet.

CONTROLLING YOUR LIFE STYLE

●

● *ARE YOU WORRIED?* If so, talk your worry over with someone you can trust like a friend or relative. You'll find that it will help you to see your problems more clearly and perhaps begin to do something about them.

● *DO YOU FEEL UNDER TENSION?* If you do, then try and change your surroundings or your daily pattern even if it's only for a short time. Afterwards you'll feel stronger and able to think more clearly about solving difficulties.

● *DO YOU GET ANGRY EASILY?* If you know you are someone who easily loses their temper, try using this energy to take a long walk or play a game. In this way you will be able to control your anger instead of increasing the tension.

● *DO YOU FEEL LONELY?* You should try doing something for someone else even if it's only smiling at them! You'll discover that it will stop you thinking about yourself for a few moments and you might begin to make more friends.

● *HAVE YOU GOT TOO MUCH TO DO?* Then try to deal with one thing at a time. Choose the urgent jobs first and forget about the others until you have more time. By the time you get round to doing these other jobs they will seem much easier.

● *ARE YOU ALWAYS TIRED?* Perhaps you're not getting enough sleep. Perhaps you are watching too much television or not getting enough fresh air. Try going for a walk or taking some regular outdoor exercise.

● *ARE YOU AFRAID OF THE FUTURE?* Plan on doing things, organise your life and keep busy and you won't have time to think what may lie ahead.

		TRUE	FALSE
21	If you are worried you should see your doctor.		
22	Altering your routine helps reduce tension.		
23	Taking physical exercise helps control a bad temper.		
24	Concentrating on your problems helps overcome loneliness.		
25	If you are overworked you should take a holiday.		
26	Tiredness is the result of too much exercise.		
27	Being fully occupied helps reduce fears over the future.		
28	Watching television helps people relax.		
29	You would find this information in a diary.		
30	The purpose of this leaflet is to give advice.		

Make these words into nouns by adding a suffix:

-ation   -tion   -ion   -ment

E.g.   alter   *alteration*

31   cancel   ....

32   improve   ....

33   select   ....

34   inform   ....

35   intend   ....

Make these words into their opposites by using a prefix:

in-   im-   un-

E.g.   sufficient   *insufficient*

36   polite   ....

37   connected   ....

38   kind   ....

39   secure   ....

40   patient   ....

Focus on writing

TEENAGERS in Britain have followed the Thatcher ethic and are working for their pocket money.

But while they are earning they are looking to the future, and dreaming of lives as pop stars, sporting heroes and policemen.

A survey shows that more than half want to stay on at school, with boys anxious to follow the Prime Minister's advice and become engineers, and girls aiming for an office job.

Many want to be PM for a day - and girls would like to be Kylie Minogue.

One out of five would choose to swap places with the Neighbours star, who has seen chart success with the girl's heart-throb, Jason Donovan. Boys saw themselves as sporting heroes or following in the dancing steps of millionaire chart star Michael Jackson, but others said they would like to spend 24 hours as a Russian or an Ethiopian.

Nearly 7,000 teenagers took part in the Halifax Building Society survey. Eight out of 10 receive regular pocket money, ranging from £2 at 12 to £9 at 16.

The average is around £3.50 a week with 30 per cent prepared to roll their sleeves up and work for a bit extra.

Paper rounds are the most common jobs at 42 per cent, followed by 17 per cent working in shops.

Around nine per cent of the youngest children claim to have a part-time job – earning on average £5.68 a week – while 53 per cent of 16-year-olds worked for an average £14.19.

Most of the cash goes on clothes, magazines and records, but 60 per cent save for gifts and holidays.

1   Write two sentences which summarise the main points of this article, as if for a NEWS IN BRIEF report.

....

....

....

....

2 Read the story 'Man of Mystery' and then summarise the information using about 70 words.

Man of Mystery

On 26 May, 1828, a teenage boy arrived in the city of Nuremberg, now in West Germany. He was wearing tattered clothes and his boots were so ill-fitting that his toes stuck out and were bleeding badly. He could hardly stand and he could say only a few words. When questioned, all he could reply were the words: 'Don't know'. However, he managed to write his name on a piece of paper - it was KASPAR HAUSER.

Hauser became an instant celebrity and people flocked to see him at the police station where he was being kept. He was taught to read and write and proved to be such a fast learner that within two weeks he was able to give a full description of his early life.

Hauser had, he said, spent all his early life locked in a small dungeon. He had no contact with the outside world and never saw his captors. One day, a man came into his cell and showed him how to write his name. He was then released. He could not remember how he had arrived in Nuremberg.

Hauser's death, five years after his arrival at Nuremberg, was as mysterious as his life had been. On 14 December, 1833, he staggered into a house with severe wounds. He claimed he had been attacked by a stranger in the park. When the Police went to investigate, they found just one set of footprints in the snow - they were Hauser's. Three days later he died, and the secret of whether his story was true or an elaborate lie died with him.

....
....
....
....
....
....
....
....
....
....

3 You are going to enter a competition to win a free trip to Britain.
You have to write a letter about yourself, your hopes and ambitions
and what you see yourself doing in ten years from now. Write between
200 and 250 words.

....

....

....

....

....

....

....

....

....

....

....

....

....

....

....

....

....

....

....

....

....

You are going to enter a competition to win a free trip to Britain.................................

Focus on listening

Listen to Frances, Deborah and Robert talking about their families. Put a tick (✔) in the box if you think a statement is correct.

Frances

Deborah

Robert

Frances'

1   grandmother was Russian. ☐

2   ancestors arrived in Ireland at the end of the 19th century. ☐

3   ancestors were musicians. ☐

4   mother did not feel at home in Ireland. ☐

Deborah's grandmother

5   died a long time ago. ☐

6   had more than ten children. ☐

7   wore her hair in a short plait. ☐

8   used her plait to protest against her husband's behaviour. ☐

> **plait** /plæt/, **plaits, plaiting, plaited. 1** If you **plait** three or more lengths of hair or rope together, you twist them over and under each other to make one thick length. EG *Her thick brown hair was plaited in a single braid down her back...*
>
> **2** A **plait** is a length of hair or rope that has been plaited. EG *...her long gold plaits, each tied with a red ribbon.*

Robert

9   knew both his grandfathers. ☐

10   says his grandfathers belonged to small families. ☐

11   had a grandfather who used to exaggerate everything. ☐

12   had a grandfather who was a sailor. ☐   ☐

For questions **13** and **14** listen to Richard and Helena talking about their ambitions and write short notes below to complete the information.

13 Richard has two main ambitions:

firstly...

....

secondly ....

....

14 Helena also has two main ambitions:

She would like ....

....

and ....

....

Answer Keys and Mark Scheme

Level 1 Test 1

Focus on vocabulary and pronunciation

Total 26 marks

1 mark for each correct answer

1   secretary   person   student   woman
2   Monday   Tuesday   Wednesday   Thursday   Friday   Saturday
3   **(a)** married   **(b)** told   **(c)** best
4   brother   father   husband   wife   daughter
5   D   9   light
6   C   10 nice
7   light   11 like
8   light   12 north

Focus on grammar

Total 11 marks

1 mark for each correct answer

1   There are
2   Where's
3   There's
4   There's
5   both
6   a   it   an   The   a   in

Focus on reading

Total 5 marks

½ mark for each correct answer

1   t   7   nt
2   nt   8   nt
3   nt   9   t
4   t   10 t
5   nt
6   nt

Focus on writing

Total 13 marks

1   Allow up to 3 marks for satisfactory completion of the task.

> MARCO'S MARRIED WITH ISABELLA.
> THEY'VE GOT THREE CHILDREN:
> TWO GIRLS AND A BABY,
> PEDRO.

3 marks. Acceptable, despite underlined error.

2 Allow up to 4 marks for satisfactory completion of the task.

> MARCO HAS GOT A WATCH, A
> KEYS, A PEN, SOME COINS,
> A PENCILS, SOME POUNDS

2 marks. Marks lost for sentence construction and confused use of article + singular/plural.

3 Allow 1 mark for each point satisfactorily made.

> THE NUMBERS AREN'T SAMES
> THERE'RE PEOPLE IN THE FIRST HOUSE
> ALSO, IT HAS ONE WINDOW MORE
> IN THE SECOND, THERE'S NOT A TREE
> THE FIRST DOOR IS OPEN.

5 marks.

Focus on listening

Total 15 marks

1

ASCHEHOUG	1 mark (correct spelling essential).
BEATRIX	1 mark (correct spelling essential).
315	½ mark for fully correct answer.
New Road	½ + ½
BS9 2LR	½ mark for fully correct answer.
46022	1 mark.

2 1 mark for each correct answer as indicated below; deduct a mark for each incorrect answer.

(a) House   (b) 4   (c) Kitchen Dining Room Living Room Bathroom

(d) —   (e) Garden Garage   (f) near train station

Level 1 Test 2

Focus on vocabulary and pronunciation

Total 17 marks

1 mark for each correct answer

1
8,853	almost nine thousand
3,002	about three thousand
407	just over four hundred
476	under five hundred
1,169	over a thousand

2 place

3 look

4 look

5 myself

6 get

7 looks

8 got

9 place

10 Get

11 yourself

12 (a) each   (b) floor

Focus on grammar

Total 14½ marks

½ mark for each correct answer for 1-11

1	must	**7**	how
2	may/might	**8**	Who
3	would	**9**	when
4	will	**10**	Which
5	where	**11**	which
6	What		

1 mark for each correct answer

12	for	**17**	at
13	by	**18**	of
14	to	**19**	to
15	at	**20**	too
16	with		

Focus on reading

Total 6½ marks

1 mark for each correct answer

1 G   **2** C   **3** D   **4** E

½ mark for each correct answer

5	nt	**7**	nt	**9**	t
6	t	**8**	nt		

Focus on writing

Total 18 marks

1 Allow up to 4 marks for satisfactory completion of the task + 4 marks for accurate use of language.

2 Allow up to 5 marks for satisfactory completion of the task + 5 marks for accurate use of language.

See sample answers to Level 1 Test 1 (page 74-75) for guidance.

Focus on listening

Total 7 marks

1 mark for each correct answer and correctly marked route on map

1 Mary   621734   after

2 November 22(nd)/twenty-second

3 **(a)** between 5 and 6/5 to 6   **(b)** Friday

4

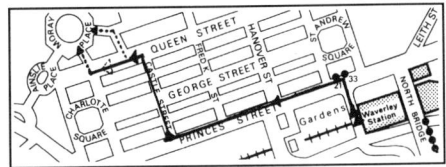

Level 1 Test 3

Focus on vocabulary

Total 12 marks

1 mark for each correct answer

1	over	**7**	keep
2	see	**8**	life
3	life	**9**	keep
4	see	**10**	over
5	over	**11**	coast
6	see	**12**	useful Europe you unusual

Focus on grammar

Total 24 marks

1 mark for each correct answer for 1-8

1 answered gave came heard was felt tried explained

2 My father is staying with us at present. (allow for variations)

3 What time did you arrive this morning?

4 have

5	have	**7**	haven't
6	had	**8**	hasn't

½ mark for each correct answer for 9-13

9   doesn't it

10   couldn't it

11   is it

12   is it

13   haven't you

1 mark for each correct sentence for 14-18

½ mark for each correct 19-21

19   —

20   (that)

21   —

Focus on reading

Total 3 marks

½ mark for each correct answer

1	nt	4	t
2	nt	5	nt
3	t	6	nt ?

Focus on writing

Total 18 marks

1   1 mark for satisfactory completion of each column. (3 marks)
    up to 5 marks for satisfactory completion of task + accuracy.

2   up to 5 marks for satisfactory completion of task in message/note form.
    up to 5 marks for accurate use of language.

See sample answers to Level 1 Test 1 (page 74-75) for guidance.

Focus on listening

Total 9 marks

1 mark for each number in correct order

1   6, 1 (supplied), 9 (supplied), 4, 2, 8, 3, 7, 5 (supplied). (6 marks)

2   **(a)** t   **(b)** nt   **(c)** nt   **(d)** t   **(e)** t   **(f)** t (½ × 6 marks)

Level 2 Test 1

Focus on vocabulary

Total 15 marks

1 mark for each correct answer

1	bit	9	time
2	time	10	about
3	look up	11	clear
4	about	12	time
5	clearly	13	spend
6	work out	14	clear
7	about	15	time
8	bit		

Focus on grammar

Total 35½ marks

1 mark for each correct answer

1   beside/near/next to   in front of   on
    above/over   under

2   was

3   are

4   is

5   Are

6   were

7   What time shall we leave?

9   Why are you sitting here by yourself?

10   Where do you live?

11   How many days until the end of term?

12   which   who   which   who

13   Have

14   had

15   having

16   Has

17   has

½ mark for 18-22

18   anything

19   Anyone

20   anyone

21   Nobody

22   Somebody

1 mark for each correct answer

23 so   but   and   but   so   and

24 This poem was written by Michael Rosen.

25 JF Kennedy was born in 1917. (allow variation)

26 The hotel is run by the Baxter family.

27 A tunnel is being built between France
and England. (allow variation)

Focus on reading

Total 7 marks

½ mark for each correct answer

1	—	6	√	11	√
2	√	7	—	12	—
3	—	8	—	13	—
4	—	9	—	14	√
5	—	10	—		

Focus on writing

Total 20 marks

1 Allow up to 5 marks for satisfactory completion of the task + 5 marks for accuracy of language.

> Dear Julia,
>
> I'm in Miami beach, This is a beautiful place and the weather here's very sunny. I'm going to come back next saturday at 9:40. I hope you are going to meet me when I arrive.

Task 5 marks +
Language 4 marks.

2 Allow up to 5 marks for satisfactory completion of the task + 5 marks for accuracy of language.

> I am a man of 50 years old, My character is open and friendly. I am interested in history, in classical music and wild life an protection of Nature. My hobby is to do jogging and long walks on the mountains. I am Proffesor of Botany in Valencia University. I teach Vegetable Ecology an research about the vegetation in Mediterranean Region.
> My ambition for the future is full time research about the vegetation in Mediterranean coast, theirs problems of conservation and protection for save this important ecosistem.

Task 5 marks + Language 3 marks.

Focus on listening

Total 7 marks

1 mark for each correct answer in question 1

1   C√   B√

½ mark for each correct answer in 2 (a-j)

2   **(a)** √   **(b)** —   **(c)** —   **(d)** —   **(e)** —   **(f)** √   **(g)** —   **(h)** √   **(i)** —   **(j)** —

Level 2 Test 2

Focus on vocabulary

Total 12 marks

1 mark for each correct answer

1	D	7	D
2	D	8	B
3	B	9	C
4	A	10	B
5	C	11	C
6	A	12	D

Focus on grammar

Total 20½ marks

1 mark for each correct completion for 1-5

1 mark for each correct answer for 6-13

6	up	10	up
7	by	11	by
8	below	12	behind
9	off	13	off

½ mark for each correct answer for 14-18

14 whatever
15 whatever
16 however
17 whoever
18 Wherever

½ mark for each correct answer

19 pull
20 had
21 promise
22 calling
23 could
24 as . . . as
25 for
26 as
27 to
28 for

Focus on reading

Total 9 marks

½ mark for each correct answer for 1-10

1 —
2 —
3 √
4 —
5 —
6 √
7 —
8 √
9 —
10 —

1 mark for each correct answer 11-14

11 C
12 D
13 B
14 D

Focus on writing

Total 20 marks

1 Allow up to 5 marks for satisfactory completion of the task + 5 marks for accuracy of language.

2 As above. See sample answers to Level 2 Test 1 (page 78) for guidance.

Focus on listening

Total 13 marks

1 mark for each box correctly filled in

1	Spain	India	Greece
	fly/plane	bus	train and ferry
	August	July	June
	camp(ing)	bed and breakfast	(cheap) hotel

1 mark for correct answer

2 C√

Level 2 Test 3

Focus on vocabulary

Total 10 marks

1	D	7	D
2	B	8	B
3	D	9	A
4	A	10	A
5	C		
6	B		

Focus on grammar

Total 20 marks

1	into	6	after
2	from	7	over
3	out	8	from
4	down	9	of . . . into
5	of	10	1 mark each for any correct answer.

11	told	14	told
12	say	15	telling
13	ask		

16 . . . it's one of the best books ever written.

17 . . . that he wanted to check my car tyres.

18 . . . her handbag had been stolen.

19 . . . the weather was cold it was bright.

20 . . . being/the fact that he was/
an old man he still walked ten miles a day.

21	U
22	C
23	U
24	U
25	C

Focus on reading

Total 18 marks

1	√
2	√
3	—
4	√
5	—
6	—

7	B
8	C
9	D
10	A
11	snatch origin evil hardly anybody similarly an instant
12	catch sight of dangerous a number of refuse enemy

Focus on writing

Total 20 marks

1   Allow up to 5 marks for satisfactory completion of task + 5 marks for accuracy of language.

2   As above. See sample answers to Level 2 Test 1 (page 78) for guidance.

Focus on listening

Total 9 marks

1	c
2	d
3	c
4	a
5	watch £200/two hundred 10/ten camera kitchen window

Level 3 Test 1

Focus on vocabulary

Total 15 marks

1 mark for each correct answer

1   retirement
2   personality
3   complaint
4   introduction
5   imaginative
6   manager/ess
7   observation
8   knowledge
9   satisfaction
10 administrator
11 non-alcoholic
12 non-smoking
13 non-stop
14 non-existent
15 non-violent

Focus on grammar

Total 28 marks

1 mark for each correct answer 1-10

1   a
2   the
3   —
4   the
5   an   the
6   took
7   put
8   did
9   went
10 taken

½ mark for each correct answer 11-20

11	used to	17	Don't
12	would	18	do
13	had to	19	do
14	used to	20	Do
15	would		
16	don't		

1 mark for each correct answer 21-32

21	out	25	a learner driver
22	over	26	a dinner party
23	up	27	a car engine
24	off	28-32	1 mark for each correct completion.

Focus on reading and dictionary skills

Total 18 marks

1 mark for each correct word or phrase correctly matched

1   customary   —   traditional
    choosing   —   picking
    generation   —   people who have lived at different times
    method   —   particular way
    a serious matter — an important event
    a common belief —   something generally thought to be true
    pretend to   —   act as though they
    go about   —   walk around
    safe   —   all right

½ mark for questions 2-9

2   —
3   —
4   √
5   —
6   √
7   —
8   —
9   √

1 mark for each correctly matched definition for 10-14

2 You refer to a work of art or a document as an **original** when it is genuine and not a copy. EG *The original is in the British Museum.* ▸ used as an adjective. EG ...*working on original documents.*

nightmare /ˈnaɪtmɛə/, **nightmares.** A night-mare is 1 a very frightening dream. EG *He rushed to her room when she had nightmares and comforted her.* **2** a very frightening or unpleasant

assume /əˈsjuːm/, **assumes, assuming, assumed. 1** If you **assume** that something is true, you imagine that it is true, sometimes wrongly. EG *I assume you don't drive... I was mistakenly assumed to be a Welshman because of my surname.*

seldom /ˈsɛldəm/. If something **seldom** happens, it happens only occasionally. EG *It seldom rains there... The waiting time was seldom less than four hours... He seldom feels confident.*

6 If you **train** for a sports match or a race, you prepare for it by doing exercises and eating a special diet.

Focus on writing

Total 14 marks

1 ½ mark for appropriate punctuation at the points indicated with a /. The sample below is marked up for guidance only and there are obviously many variables. Maximum 4 marks.

I was packing a few sandwiches and some drink all into my rucksack / snow was falling steadily outside and the grass looked like icing on a cake / the howling rain and wind nearly put us off / but we still went out / the moon rising over the pine trees made the whole scene look very romantic / then when I looked up to the sky I saw lots of broken clouds / one of them like a young girl / another a man running and another a bird of prey swooping down /

2 Allow up to 5 marks for satisfactory completion of the task + 5 marks for accuracy of language.

> I have read your advertisement. I am interested in the job you are offering. I am a student at Oxford and I'd like to work during the period between June and September. I know very well Venice because I was born there and I spent a few years of my life there. I have already worked as a holiday guide and you can obtain references from the travel agency I used to work for in the past. I speak fluently German and French and, of course, Italian which is my mother tongue. My address is 38 Oxford Road, Faringdon
> Yours

Task 5 marks + Language 4 marks.

Focus on listening

Total 7½ marks

1 mark for each correct answer

1 leather   for/with father/in father's business

English   likes England/English people/way of life   being alone/skiing/walking

½ mark for each correct answer

2 (a) —   (b) —   (c) √   (d) √   (e) √   (f) —

Level 3 Test 2

Focus on vocabulary

Total 20 marks

1 mark for each correct answer

1	give	**7**	tied
2	put/get	**8**	actresses/actors
3	giving	**9**	inconvenient
4	get	**10**	nationality
5	held	**11**	passionate
6	good — evil	**12**	Racial
	harmless — deadly	**13**	conservation
	death — birth	**14**	scarcely
	enemy — friend	**15**	campaigner
	comedy — tragedy	**16**	effective
	loose — tight		

Focus on grammar

Total 27½ marks

1 mark for each correct completion for 1-5
1 mark for each correct answer 1-25

6 which
7 whose
8 which
9 where
10 whose
11 more . . . more
12 better
13 more
14 less
15 more . . . less
16 . . . the train being late, I still arrived on time.
17 . . . the rain/the fact that it was raining.
18 . . . I could drive.
19 . . . I had not got married.
20 . . . bought Jim's car for £1000.
21 (any correct using 'had').
22 . . . can't/couldn't have . . .
23 . . . should/ought to . . .
24 . . . would/might have been . . .
25 . . . could/might/may have . . .

½ mark for each correct 26-30

26 doesn't it   **29** hasn't she
27 would it   **30** mustn't it
28 wasn't it

Focus on reading and dictionary skills

Total 12½ marks

1 mark for each correct answer

1	out	**4**	made
2	the	**5**	a
3	or	**6**	but

½ mark for 7-11

7	√	**10**	√
8	—	**11**	—
9	√		

1 mark for 12-15

12	C	**14**	A
13	C	**15**	D

Focus on writing

Total 16 marks

1 Up to 2 marks for each piece of advice.
2 Allow up to 5 marks for satisfactory completion of task + 5 marks for accuracy of language.
See Level 3 Test 1 (page 82) for sample answers.

Focus on listening

Total 6 marks

½ mark for each correct answer

1	—	**8**	—
2	√	**9**	√
3	—	**10**	√
4	—	**11**	√
5	√	**12**	—
6	—		
7	√		

Level 3 Test 3

Focus on vocabulary

Total 12 marks

1 mark for each correct answer

1 consideration
2 psychological
3 responsibility
4 rapidly
5 developments
6 representatives
7 cultural
8 protesters
9 shortage
10 reliable
11 politician
12 destruction

Focus on grammar

Total 25 marks

1 mark for each correct answer

1 in (allow under/beneath)
2 from
3 of
4 from
5 to
6 ... see the world is to hitch-hike.
7 ... he would get married.
8 ... nine hour hourney from London to Aberdeen.
9 ... you had asked my permission before borrowing my car I would not have been so angry.
10 ... I known you were going to the cinema I would have gone with you.

1 mark for each correct completion for 11-15

1 mark for each correct answer

16 dependent
17 compete
18 level
19 proposed
20 equal/equality
21 how
22 where
23 what
24 which
25 who(m)

Focus on reading and dictionary skills

Total 16 marks

1 mark for each correctly matched headline and text

1   D

2   C

3   E

4   A

5   B

1 mark for each correct position

6   D, B, C, A, E

½ mark for 7-10

7   —

8   √

9   √

10 √

1 mark for 11-14

11 farmer

12 broadcast

13 lose

14 dim

Focus on writing

Total 31½ marks

½ mark for each correct change and addition as underlined

1   I am writing to complain about the packet of biscuits which I bought from/at/in your store last week.
    When I opened the packet I found a piece of metal inside.
    It was fortunate I did not swallow it.
    I am enclosing/I enclose the piece of metal together with the receipt for the biscuits.
    I look forward to hearing from you as soon as possible.

2   Allow up to 5 marks for satisfactory completion of the task + 5 marks for accuracy of language.

3   Allow up to 2 marks for satisfactory completion of the task + 2 marks for accuracy of language.

4   As **3** above.

See Level 3 Test 1 (page 82) for sample answers.

Focus on listening

Total 12 marks

1   textbook

2   periodically/sometimes

3   3 months

4   seminar programmes

7   telephoning

8   books

5   too many places/exhausting

6   to Spain

9   materials

10 coloured tags on luggage

11 opera in Belgrade

12 Banquet

Level 3 Test 4

Focus on vocabulary

Total 20 marks

1	D	**8**	A	**15**	C
2	B	**9**	C	**16**	D
3	C	**10**	B	**17**	B
4	A	**11**	D	**18**	C
5	D	**12**	C	**19**	B
6	B	**13**	B	**20**	D
7	C	**14**	A		

Focus on grammar

Total 20 marks

1 mark for each correct sentence (allow for variations)

1 ... glanced up nervously at the policeman.
2 The trip was unfortunately cancelled ...
3 ... unusually serious as she entered the room.
4 It was pretty silly of you to go sailing ...
5 ... carefully lifted the injured man onto the bed.

1 mark for each correct completion for 6-10 and adequate (if poorly) expressed explanation for 11-15

11 is a party to which mainly members of your family are invited.
12 is a large ring used to keep a person afloat and prevent them from drowning when they fall into deep water.
13 are special clothes worn when you take part in sports.
14 are guards whose job it is to check people at frontiers between countries.
15 is a room specially set aside for people to smoke in.
16 in case of
17 unless
18 but
19 as/because/since/for
20 Although

Focus on reading and dictionary skills

Total 35 marks

1 mark for each correct answer

1 it
2 to
3 off
4 the
5 has
6 permission/clearance
7 called/named
8 height
9 top
10 the
11 blows/pushes
12 wrong
13 would
14 in
15 All
16 from
17 there
18 being
19 of
20 until

½ mark for each correct answer 21-30

21	F	**26**	F
22	T	**27**	T
23	T	**28**	F
24	F	**29**	F
25	F	**30**	T

1 mark for each answer correctly spelt

31 cancellation
32 improvement
33 selection
34 information
35 intention
36 impolite
37 unconnected
38 unkind
39 insecure
40 impatient

Focus on writing

Total 38 marks

1 Allow 2 marks for each sentence: 1 for content + 1 for expression (4 marks).

2 Allow 1 mark for each point made up to a maximum of 10.

Allow for variations in order.

1 (May 26th) 1828 a boy – wearing old clothes

2 Very exhausted/tired

3 Arrived Nuremburg (West Germany)

4 Name – Kasper Hauser

5 He could hardly speak

6 He learnt to read and write (become very famous)

7 Lived all early life in cell/dungeon

8 Died 5 years later

9 He said he had been attacked by stranger

10 Police could only find his footsteps in snow!

Allow up to 4 marks for expression and coherent linking.

3 Allow up to 20 marks: 10 for content + 10 for letter form and accuracy of language.

See Level 3 Test 1 (page 82) for sample answers.

Focus on listening

Total 14 marks

½ mark for each correct answer

1 √

2 √

3 —

4 —

5 —

6 √

7 —

8 √

9 √

10 —

11 √

12 √

1 mark for each correct point made (ignore irrelevant material)

13 firstly: spend more time/live in Wales.

work in Welsh.

secondly: develop theatre company so that it is full-time.

tour schools.

get money for the theatre/expand theatre.   (5 marks)

14 She would like: to spend more time with charity which is trying to find a cure for skin condition.

would like to travel abroad/see other countries.

and: enjoy work/make enough money/live comfortably.   (3 marks)

Transcripts

Level 1 Test 1

M1: Winscombe School of English, can I help you? Yes. Can I have your name please? Yes, your surname. Can you say that again? Aha. That's A-S-C-H-E-H-O-U-G. Right? And your first name, please. Mhm mhm. That's B-E-A-T-R-I-X. Er, can you give me your address? Yes. Three one five, New Road, Bristol BS9 2LR. Erm, can you give me your phone number? Four six 0 double two. Yes, certainly. Yes, I'll ....

M2: Hello, can I help you?
F1: Yes, I hope so. I'm looking for a house. Erm, somewhere near the town centre, if possible. Four bedrooms –
M2: Mhm.
F1: – kitchen, bathroom – nice sized bathroom if possible – dining room, living room...
M2: Mhm.
F1: Erm, I want as – a house, as I said, rather than a flat.
M2: Mhm mhm.
F1: Old, not modern.
M2: Mhm mhm.
F1: Not too many stairs. And I'd really like good windows, plenty of light. Erm, and the garden needs to be quite big.
M2: Yep. Okay.
F1: Yes. Erm, garage if possible. And again if possible near the train station.
M2: Fairly near?
F1: Yeah, well, you know, within reasonable walking distance.
M2: Right.

Level 1 Test 2

M1: Hello.
F1: Oh, hi. Can I speak to Ann please?
M1: Oh, sorry. I'm afraid she's out. Can I take a message?
F1: Oh, er, right. Ye- yes please. Er, my name's Mary. Erm, could you ask her to, erm, phone me after work tomorrow? My – my number's six two one seven three four.
M1: Six two one seven three four. Okay. I'll leave her a note.
F1: Oh, thanks ever so much.
M1: She shouldn't be long anyway.
F1: Thank you.
M1: Okay.
F1: Bye bye.
M1: Bye bye.

F1: By the way, can you tell me when Howard's birthday is?

F2: Oh, November the twenty-second.
F1: No, really! That's the same as mine! Mine's November the twenty-second too!

M1: Okay, fine. Thanks John. But when's the best time to get you at home?
M2: Er, well, usually between five and six in the evening. Oh, except Friday this week.
M1: Okay, I'll call you after I get home on Thursday evening. Is that all right?
M2: Mhm, fine.
M1: I shouldn't be too late. It's just that I'm going out to the, er..........

F1: [ON PHONE] It's really very easy. Come out of Waverley Station, and turn right up to Princes Street, to the traffic lights. Er, cross that road there and then turn left down Princes Street. You want to take Castle Street, which is – one, two, three – the fourth turning on the right. Now go straight up Castle Street, and then you'll meet Queen Street. Turn left into Queen Street and one of the turnings on the right, any one of those turnings on the right and you'll come to Moray Place, no problem. All right?

Level 1 Test 3

F1: Oh, hello, Karl. You're back early.
M1: Hello, Mrs Johnson.
F1: How did it go? Have you had a good day?
M1: Yes. Thanks, yes, it was all right.
F1: Only all right! Well what have you been doing? Have a seat and tell me all about it.
M1: Oh, yes, right. Well, first of all when I got there – after you'd left – we went to a very large room, er, the – the students' room, where you have your coffee break. And, er, all the other students were there. And then some of the teachers came in and introduced themselves, so we all had a chance to meet them. Then one of the teachers told us about the arrangements for the day. And then we went to our classroom. I'm in a – a really nice classroom. It's quite big, with lots of pictures on the walls. And then we had a test –
F1: Oh!
M1: – but it was quite easy. Erm, and then after that we had coffee and I met some of the students from the – from the other classes. And then we had to stay in the students' room to see a video –
F1: A video!
M1: Yes, a video about some of the places we'll be going to this term – like, er, Oxford, Windsor, Stratford –
F1: Oh, that'll be nice!
M1: And then we had lunch, which wasn't very good, but, er, perhaps it'll be better tomorrow! Then we went to get our, er, our textbooks. Er, we got out textbooks, and out teacher, Miss Fox, gave us our homework for this evening.

F1: Homework already!
M1: Yes, so I – I think we're going to be working quite hard ....

[TELEPHONE ANSWERING MACHINE]
F1: Hi, Sue, it's Lisa. You're never going to believe this, but I – I'm coming to England next week. At long last! Look – erm, I'm arriving on Thursday the twenty-fifth. Oh, what am I talking about, the – Wednesday the twenty-fifth. Erm, I'm – I'm going to stay with my brother for a week in London and then I was thinking of going to Edinburgh to see Rosa. Er, I wonder if we could meet up, maybe up in London or I could if – if you're – if you're too busy I could come down to Exeter bef – before I go to Edinburgh. Erm, do you think you can ring me later today? Erm, I'll be home about ten o'clock. Ten – ten o'clock tonight. All right, hope to speak to you later. Bye!

Level 2 Test 1

F3: Police are looking for a man and a woman in their early twenties who broke into a jewellers shop in the early hours of this morning. The alarm was raised by people working in the bakery opposite who heard the breaking of glass. Two people were seen running away. The man is described as being very tall and well-built, with dark hair which is fairly long and untidy-looking. The woman with him is described as being small and slim with short fair hair cut very close to her head. She was wearing jeans and a leather jacket. Anyone who has any information or can give further details ....

F4: ... thanks, I'll be able to buy you a coffee next time – I get paid tomorrow! At long last. Honestly it's been like being a student again, no money to do anything.
M3: Don't worry, it's always like this when you start your first job. In a few months you won't know what to do with your money!
F4: Huh. You don't know what it's like.
M3: Yes I do. You've forgotten. I had some really awful jobs for about six months before I got a good job and ...
F4: Oh yeah, I remember. Didn't you work in a hotel or something?
M3: Yeah, in the kitchen, washing up and preparing the vegetables. It was terrible and the chef was so bad-tempered, shouting at everyone all the time. And then after a month I was asked to leave!
F4: Why?
M3: Well the manager said I was too slow – and I said to him that the floor was so greasy that it was dangerous to move quickly and he told me to get out! So then I worked in a factory for a while which I also hated. They packed flour and dried soup and things like that for hotels and whatnot, great big tins and boxes and when I'd finished each day I was absolutely covered in dust and stuff. It made me cough and sneeze all the time as well. I felt so ill – I just went home each night feeling awful. Anyway after a week I couldn't stand it so I took myself off to a job centre, and they sent me to work in an office. I can't remember what sort of office but it was boring beyond

description, boring boring boring, and the pay was awful. I thought I'd never get a job which I enjoyed and which paid reasonably well. And then suddenly I got this offer from a company that I'd written to months before and I'd never had a reply, and they wrote and said they needed someone who could speak German and French in their sales section. And that was it. From rags to riches! Well, not exactly riches, but I'm well-paid, and by this time next year I should be earning even more, so who's complaining ....

Level 2 Test 2

M4: ... do you want another cup of coffee?
F2: No, I'm okay thanks. Shall we get down to planning this holiday?
M4: Yeah, right. Erm, I've brought some brochures with me.
F2: Oh good, let's have a look. Oh, look at that – that looks gorgeous.
M4: Mhm? Where is it?
F2: Portugal somewhere.
M4: No, I don't want to go to Portugal. I went there last year.
F2: So where do you want to go then?
M4: Well I'd like to go somewhere exotic – India for example.
F2: India! No, that's too far. I'd like to go to Spain.
M4: No thank you. Okay, if India's too far how about Greece? I've never been there.
F2: Mhm, won't it be terribly hot?
M4: Well, so would Spain!
F2: Mhm, I suppose so. All right, Greece. But let's go to an island, a really deserted island where we can just lie around on a beach all day.
M4: Are we going to fly?
F2: Of course! What were you thinking of doing? Walking?
M4: No, it's just that – well, there are some really cheap fares if you go by bus.
F2: But it'd take ages!
M4: About two days. You sleep on the bus and travel overnight.
F2: Oh, I'd hate that, cooped up with all those people, unable to get up and stretch your legs for hours on end.
M4: Okay then, let's compromise. Let's go by train and get a ferry to one of the islands.
F2: Done. So we'll need to book. Now, when are we going? I'd like to go in August.
M4: Mhm, I can't manage August because my brother's coming to stay. How about July? That would suit me.
F2: No, sorry, I'm tied up.
M4: Well I don't want to go in September, so how about June then?
F2: Yeah, that's fine. Warm but not too hot. And are we going to camp like we did when we went to France? That was great. I love camping. Let's camp again this time.
M4: Oh no, I know it's cheap, but the thought of not having a nice cool room – let's try and find bed and breakfast.
F2: But sometimes you can't go back during the day and they want you out early in the morning. Let's try and find a cheap hotel.
M4: Well it'll have to be cheap, mind you, but I must

say a hotel would be nice.

Level 2 Test 2

F3: [IN TELEPHONE BOX] Hello Sarah, it's me. Look, I'm sorry, but I'm going to be late. No, it's not that. Yes, I am using the map you sent me but I'm lost, completely lost. I haven't a clue where I am. Okay. Well look, I'll tell you where I am, then perhaps you can tell me! I'm in a call box by some crossroads. Well, I've been driving along that A39 for simply ages and I – I've just passed a large garage. Yeah, that's right. There are some shops opposite. No, no I can't see one ... oh hang on ... yes, I can, just beyond the garage. Yes, got it. Oh, so I'm not that far away. Okay, back down the A39 and turn right beside the church. Yes ... fine. See you shortly then! Thanks.

Level 2 Test 3

[LOST LUGGAGE OFFICE]

M3: Can I help you?
F4: Yes, yes I've lost my bag. I left it on the bus. Has anyone handed it in?
M3: Well, we've had quite a few in, can you tell me what it's like?
F4: Yes, it's quite big, black leather with a gold letter A on the side.
M3: Right you are, I'll have a look for you ...

[HOTEL RECEPTION]

F3: I'd like to book a room for tonight, please.
F2: Erm, we've very few beds left.
F3: It's just for me.
F2: Right, I can offer you a room on the first floor, eighteen pounds including breakfast.

[CAFE]

M4: Do you know any tricks?
F4: Erm, I can do that one with matches and a glass of water.
M4: Oh go on then, show me, please!

[STREET]

M3: Oh, did you see that?
F3: What?
M3: Those big black cats, they ran straight in front of me.
F3: So?
M3: Well, it's good luck, double good luck – not just one, but two!

F2 – Police Officer; M4 – Mr Hewlett

F2: Right then, Mr Hewlett, if you'll tell me what's happened then I'll make a note.
M4: There's an awful lot missing, officer.
F2: Well it'd be a good idea if you can get round to the various second-hand shops in the area and have a look in their windows, you never know ...
M4: I'll do that this morning. You think there's a chance of finding my wife's jewellery? And my watch? My gold watch has gone.
F2: You can never tell, although in my experience most stuff finds its way into shops hundreds of miles from here. These thieves, these burglars they know what they're doing, straight onto the motorways and off. There have been a number of crimes in this area, robberies and suchlike, small stuff, rings, bracelets, earrings, cheque books, credit cards, anything that can be carried fairly easily. Anyway, I'll make a note of your watch.
M4: And cash?
F2: Right, how much cash was stolen?
M4: Two hundred pounds.
F2: That's a lot of money to have around, sir.
M4: Yes I know, but we were going to have a party tonight and the money was for today's shopping.
F2: I see, well I'm afraid you're not likely to see that again.
M4: No, I realise that. My cheque book's gone as well – there were about ten cheques left.
F2: Right.
M4: And my camera's been taken – that was worth about six hundred pounds.
F2: Where was your camera?
M4: Well, I know it sounds silly but it was in the kitchen. I never normally leave it there but I'd put a new film in last night ready for today.
F2: Yes, I understand, sir.
M4: And of course they broke in through the kitchen window.
F2: Was it locked?
M4: Yes, but the lock's been broken, looks as if the wood in the window frame was rotten. Anyway, all the wood's been hacked away, we'll have to have a new window.
F2: You'll need to get that fixed straight away. I'll send one of my men round and he'll give you some advice on what kind of lock to fix.
M4: Okay, thanks.

Level 3 Test 1

TEACHER: Okay, erm, okay. So I've asked you all here, erm, you know that each year we write a piece about the overseas students who come to study at the college and, erm, what I'd like to do is talk to each of you in turn and make a few notes so that I can write up the piece later on.
AYAKO: Can we see it before you print it?
TEACHER: Erm, yes all right, but I don't promise I'll change anything!
TEACHER: Erm, now, Oscar, why are you studying here?
OSCAR: Well, my parents thought it would be very good for me and it would help to improve my English.
TEACHER: Do you need English in Brazil?
OSCAR: Yes, very much. And when I go back to Brazil I will work in my father's company, it's a leather trading company and he exports animal skins, leather,

all over the world. So he needs me to work in the Export Department of the company and also to meet the various buyers who come to his company.

TEACHER: I see. So you'll go straight back to work for your father?

OSCAR: Not immediately. I think first of all I will go to university to study Economics or Business Management because then I will be more, I'll be better qualified.

TEACHER: That sounds like a good idea. Now what about you, Linda?

LINDA: Well, my mother's English but she's married to a Norwegian, so although I live in Norway I've always been to England for holidays and I really like the English people and the way of life.

TEACHER: Is it very different from Norway?

LINDA: Well not very different – although the food is! But English people are more friendly, more outgoing.

TEACHER: Really? You don't often hear that.

LINDA: Yes, we Norwegians are very solitary people really. There's nothing a Norwegian likes more than to walk in the mountains or go skiing for hours on end all alone, we have quite a lot of jokes about this, I'll tell you ....

Level 3 Test 1

KO: The last holiday I took was at Eastertime when I went for a five-day break to Paris, erm ...

PK: Mhm mhm.

KO: I travelled by train from London and as I say my holiday was only five days long. Erm, we went for a short sightseeing trip in Paris and we stayed ...

PK: Mhm mhm.

KO: ... in a hotel fairly near the centre. Erm, we did various things, sightseeing, as I said.

PK: Was that your first time in Paris?

KO: No, it's about the fourth time I've been in Paris. Erm, we went about to different museums and to different places of interest.

PK: Yeah.

KO: And visited a few friends.

PK: Mhm mhm. And erm, and do you think you might go again on that sort of holiday?

KO: I presume, I think we'll probably go again next year, as it's, you know, very easy to get to and there are no problems with looking at – seeing around it.

PK: Mhm. Yeah, so you, you loo – you looked around Paris and did all the sights?

KO: Yeah, normally, norm – yes, well normally when we go on holiday we like just to look around rather than go out into the country and other things and ...

PK: Yeah, yeah.

KO: ... so for me, looking round museums is the most important thing.

PK: Mhm, yeah. And, erm, how many of you were there on this holiday?

KO: Just myself and my girlfriend.

PK: Ah, I see. [ ]

KO: And so we did various things apart from sightseeing. Eating, a lot of eating, and a lot of drinking. And that's how I spent my holiday.

PK: Well, it's a very nice way to spend a holiday.

KO: Yes.

PK: Yes.

Level 3 Test 2

M3: I don't know why you're laughing, it was awful ... go on, Dot, it's your turn now, the worst thing that's ever happened to you.

DOT: Oh, there are so many! I don't know, erm, oh yes, right, I didn't tell you what happened last month on my way out to Norway – probably not the worst thing that's ever happened, but bad enough. Well, you know I was travelling on a Sunday ... so I turn up at the station and discover the train's running about half an hour late.

F4: Why?

DOT: Oh, the usual, engineering works and what-have-you. So I ask the chappie on the platform what'll happen to the connecting train to Gatwick. Oh don't worry, says he, they'll hold it. Lots of people waiting for this train are going to the airport so they'll hold it until your train arrives. Fine! So I don't worry. Until we get to Reading – that's where you pick up the connecting train – and discover that the train for the airport has already left! I couldn't believe it.

M4: Couldn't you have caught the next one?

DOT: Well that's it – there wasn't another one for over an hour! So, dragging all my luggage, I staggered along to the station master's office. I was furious. I told him what had happened and that I'd miss my plane. He says it's nothing to do with him and I'll just have to catch another plane. Which of course I can't do because I've got a cheapie ticket and you can't transfer it. Anyway there was another chap in this office, and he followed me outside and suggested I caught a bus to Heathrow.

F2: But you wanted Gatwick.

DOT: Yes, I know. But he said that there was a bus outside the station due to leave in a few minutes and there was a connecting bus service between the two airports. That way I'd probably get there quicker than waiting for the next train as the buses travelled non–stop on the motorway. Anyway, we arrived at Heathrow and off I go again, heaving all my luggage and would you believe it ...

M3: The bus had left.

DOT: Right. I could have wept. There was still about an hour and a quarter until the plane left, so I decided I'd have to get a taxi as there was no way I could afford another ticket. So I jump into a taxi and there's this nice driver who says that if I sit tight he'll get me to the airport in time. I could have kissed him! And then as I was leaning back in my seat I saw the list of charges and the fare to Gatwick was fifty-five pounds! And I only had twenty pounds on me. And it was Sunday, no banks open, etc, etc. And I didn't have a cheque book with me. I didn't know what to do. So I just sat there feeling really sick. Anyway, we got to the airport in record time and the taxi driver jumps out, grabs my bits and pieces and says 'Run – I'll bring your luggage!' So obviously I had to tell him I hadn't enough money to pay him. He looked fairly annoyed, I can tell you. I offered him the twenty pounds and then he asked me if I had any jewellery or a watch I could leave with him and he'd return them when I'd sent him the rest of the money. Which I hadn't, of course! So then I said I'd phone my husband and he'd put a cheque in the post immediately. Well he didn't like that suggestion, and meanwhile the flight is boarding and this guy's holding on to my cases and things and I'm nearly in tears! So finally he agrees and there's this mad phone call with the taxi driver yelling his name and address down the phone and then we both run for

dear life, and I get waved through Customs – by this time I'm on my own with a trolley. And there I am belting along for all I'm worth with the taxi driver shouting goodbye and I made it, I actually caught the plane! And I spent most of the flight just recovering, I couldn't stop trembling and shaking. When I got to Bergen this Norwegian says in his usual calm way, 'I hope you had a good journey'. I burst out laughing, I could have died and he looked totally bewildered, poor man, at this crazy English woman laughing herself silly at a perfectly harmless question.
M4:   Oh, that's great.

Level 3 Test 3

PRESENTER: In the studio with me this afternoon is Gillian Windlesham. She's what is known as a Specialist Tourist, a title which I must confess I'd never heard of. Gill, it sounds quite exotic ... what exactly do you do?
GW: Well I can assure you it's not at all exotic! In fact it's a bit of a misnomer, it's nothing to do with tourism at all. As you know I'm a writer, a writer of textbooks for English language teachers and periodically I get invitations from the British Council to go to various countries abroad either to give a series of lectures, or seminars or to work with teachers on a residential in-service training course.
PRESENTER: So you drop everything and off you go ...
GW: Not quite just like that. You usually get about three months' warning because very often you have to write materials specifically for the course or whatever.
PRESENTER: And do you get to exciting places?
GW: Well, it depends what you mean by exciting. I've certainly been to places which I've found quite fascinating and on a residential course where you get to know the people you're working with it can proved a very interesting insight into the life of that country. Seminar programmes, however, are less enjoyable. A different place each night, a different sea of faces each day. It can become very exhausting and of course you see virtually nothing of the country and at the end of a week I get to a point where I can't remember what I've said and to whom I've said it!
PRESENTER: So where have you actually been?
GW: Um, well in some cases I've been back to the same country quite a few times – like Norway, for example, Italy, Belgium, Finland, Portugal, Yugoslavia, Poland, Hong Kong, Greece, South America.
PRESENTER: Good heavens.
GW: And strangely enough just as I was leaving home today to come to the studio I had a phone call asking me to go to Spain, to Granada.
PRESENTER: And will you accept?
GW: Oh yes, I have already! Somewhere I've never been before.
PRESENTER: Gill, can you tell us what the planning of such a visit involves? I mean after you've said 'yes' – what then?
GW: Right. Well, usually you get the details of what you're being asked to do on paper. This form gives you the dates of the course or whatever, where it's being held, who'll be attending and how many people you can expect and so on. The bit that's really essential is the part that details what you're actually being asked to do and the subject areas that people want covered. There's usually a contact person you

can then liaise with. That means that if there's plenty of time I'll write and follow things up on paper. If not I'll telephone or maybe they'll telephone me, and you can discuss things further. The most important thing is to be absolutely clear, or as clear as you can be, about what it is you're going to be doing. Then I might have to order books or materials for the course, and I'll need to write materials myself. If I'm going to a country where I know it's difficult to get things like photocopies made, then I'll probably get all that done this end either through the Council or – or I'll take it all with me. The Council also send you background details on the country which I find very helpful – details about the political situation, the climate, culture, etc. But nothing is ever as smooth as you hope and I've turned up in countries before now and discovered that things I've ordered haven't arrived, or I've been told I'll be met at the airport and there's no one there!
PRESENTER: Oh dear.
GW: There's this lovely system of being identified by the coloured tags on one's luggage. So I stand around in airports self-conciously displaying my luggage labels in the hope that someone will rush up to me! They invariably do of course and the system works, but I always find it mildly amusing.
PRESENTER: What have been the highlights of some of your visits?
GW: Mhm, a difficult question, there have been a lot over the years. Riding on a sledge through Polish forests in freezing cold temperatures at midnight with snow piled up along the paths ... erm the opening gala night of the opera in Belgrade ... erm, an amazing banquet in Hong Kong with all kinds of food which I'd never tasted before ....

Level 3 Test 4

DM: Francis, did you – did you know your grandparents?
FJ: Yes, I did. Erm, I always remember very strongly as a child my – my grandmother came from Russia, her family came from Russia –
DM: Really? Russia!
FJ: – from St Petersburg. And they came over to Dublin, and settled in Dublin and my great grandfather started a small business and ...
RW: That's Leningrad, isn't it, St. Petersburg?
FJ: That's right, it's Leningrad now. But this was a big capital city, St. Petersburg.
DM: This was when, what, what ...
FJ: Er, this would have been at the turn of the century. And he started this business, and he did very well and I think they had quite a comfortable life. But I know my grandmother always had the sense of being an outsider. Whereas my mother, born and brought up in Ireland, felt she belonged. I mean there was a terrific –
DM: Oh right, yes –
FJ: – difference in being an immigrant and yet being born and growing up in a country. But what about you, did you know your grandparents, Deborah?
DM: Yes, I did, but erm I especially remember my father's mother, my grandmother, who in fact unfortunately died just recently but she was a wonderful lady and she was – she had quite a hard life. Erm, apparently, erm, my grandfather married beneath him and he was disinherited. But my grandmother had eleven children and after the eleventh she thought 'I've had

enough'. And at the time she used to wear this wonderful black plait all down her back – she used to be able to sit on it. And she was fed up after the eleventh child because er – it happened while erm grandpop, as we used to call him was out and about. He was a bit of a boy. And she said – she said, 'That's enough', and she got the scissors and she cut off her plait and she stuck it on the wall. So grandpop came in and – 'Oh, my goodness!'

FJ: He knew what that meant.

DM: He knew what that meant. It was an early feminist stance, I think. So what about you?

RW: Yes, erm, I – I knew three of my grandparents in fact. In fact I remember one occasion, er, overhearing a conversation between my two grandfathers, my dad's dad and my mum's dad, which I think sort of gives a good indication of – of what it was like then as compared to – to now. They both, like – like your parents, er, Deborah, came from very large families and I remember my – my dad's saying something to – something along the lines of erm – because we'd been discussing how much we earned, erm, how – or you know, and complaining about how – how we didn't think we earned very much and he was saying, 'Well, when I was young, my dad earned thirty shillings a week, and that was for eight of us'.

DM: Oh, goodness!

RW: And my other grandfather said 'Huh, well my dad only earned twenty five shillings a week, and that was for nine of us!'.

FJ: Oh Robert, gosh.

RW: I know, it's just ridiculous. 'Cause my – my mum's dad has got this thing that he has to outdo anybody for anything.

FJ: Yes.

RW: Like, er, his memories, er, are just ridiculous. I mean he ran away to sea when he was fourteen. He was the youngest of, er, nine children. All the others were girls, so perhaps that's why he ran away to sea when he was fourteen. And er, he tells me stories of having to tap the biscuits on the table to get the weevils out, which I think he's probably read is what used to happen in Nelson's time –

FJ: Oh sure, yes I –

RW: – but he – he believes it now.

FJ: It's quite a long time ago I would have thought, the weevils.

Level 3 Test 4

HB: Have you got any ambitions, Richard?

RM: Hm. Ambitions. Erm, yes, I s- – I suppose I have. Erm. They're sort of – my ambitions change every few years but I suppose they fall into two sort of categories. One, I'd like to spend more time in Wales. I bought a little cottage on the Welsh border a few years ago and I'd like to work down there more so I could live down there more. And I'd like to use my Welsh language more and do more work in Welsh. So that – that's one. Erm, that's sort of happening slowly I suppose. And the other is, I started a little theatre company a few years ago with a friend in Oxford and we do plays every summer. And I'd like – that gives me so much satisfaction I'd like that to expand into a more full-time thing and – we're going to the Edinburgh Festival this year for instance –

HB: Great! Mhm.

RM: – which will be a bit more exciting, and maybe a little tour of schools but I'd like – I'd like to be able to

get some good financial backing for that and pay people proper wages and generally expand that a bit. So those are sort of two things, really. Those are the main things.

HB: The main things.

RM: What about you, Helena, do you have any – any pipe dreams?

HB: Mhm – I – yes, yes, not so much career-wise, but erm, I'm very involved with a charity and I've got a lot of ambitions for them I suppose. Pipe dreams for them.

RM: What sort of charity?

HB: Oh it's a – it's a – it's a charity – a – a medical charity trying to find a cure for a skin condition.

RM: Aha. Yeah.

HB: And that – that would be wonderful. I would, erm, like to spend a lot more time with that.

RM: Oh, that's terrific, yeah.

HB: And er, that, that, yes, erm. I – I'd also like to travel more. Get the chance to travel more if I could. Erm, particularly abroad.

RM: Mhm.

HB: I've done very little travelling, er, very limited amount and I'd – I'd love to get the chance to – to go and see other countries and –

RM: And preferably be paid for it at the same time!

HB: – and preferably be paid for it at the same time, absolutely. Yes, but erm, yes, not – not too many ambitions career-wise apart from doing good work and enjoying the work.

RM: Yes. And working with nice people.

HB: And – yes, and, and obviously making enough money to – to live comfortably, but er –

RM: Yes.

HB: – that's probably about all, I – I would want.